Studies in Marxism and Social Theory

Alternatives to Capitalism

Studies in Marxism and Social Theory

Edited by G.A. COHEN, JON ELSTER AND JOHN ROEMER

The series is jointly published by the Cambridge University Press and the Edition de la Maison des Sciences de l'Homme, as part of the joint publishing agreement established in 1977 between the Fondation de la Maison des Sciences de l'Homme and the Syndics of the Cambridge University Press.

The books in the series are intended to exemplify a new paradigm in the study of Marxist social theory. They will not be dogmatic or purely exegetical in approach. Rather, they will examine and develop the theory pioneered by Marx, in the light of the intervening history, and with the tools of non-Marxist social science and philosophy. It is hoped that Marxist thought will thereby be freed from the increasingly discredited methods and presuppositions which are still widely regarded as essential to it, and that what is true and important to Marxism will be more firmly established.

Also in the series

Alternatives to Capitalism

edited by

Jon Elster
University of Chicago

Karl Ove Moene
University of Oslo

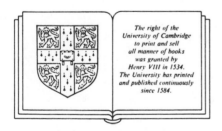

The right of the
University of Cambridge
to print and sell
all manner of books
was granted by
Henry VIII in 1534.
The University has printed
and published continuously
since 1584.

Cambridge University Press

Cambridge

New York   Port Chester   Melbourne   Sydney

Editions de la Maison des Sciences de l'Homme

Paris

Published by the Press Syndicate of the University of Cambridge
The Pitt Building, Trumpington Street, Cambridge CB2 1RP
40 West 20th Street, New York, NY 10011, USA
10 Stamford Road, Oakleigh, Melbourne 3166, Australia
and
Editions de la Maison des Sciences de l'Homme
54 Boulevard Raspail, 75270 Paris, Cedex 06, France

First published 1989
Reprinted 1990

Printed in the United States of America

Library of Congress Cataloging-in-Publication Data
Alternatives to capitalism / edited by Jon Elster and Karl Ove Moene.
p.   cm. – (Studies in Marxism and social theory)
Includes bibliographies.
1. Capitalism.   2. Socialism.   3. Central Planning.   4. Profit
sharing.   I. Elster, Jon, 1940– .   II. Moene, Karl Ove
III. Series
HB501.A558   1989
338.9 – dc19   88-30182
                                                                    CIP

British Library Cataloguing-in-Publication Data
Alternatives to Capitalism – (Studies in Marxism and
social theory)
1. Economic systems. Comparative Studies
I. Elster, Jon, 1940–   II. Moene, Karl Ove
III. Series
330.12

ISBN 2 7351 0285 8 hardback (France only)
ISBN 2 7351 0286 6 paperback (France only)
ISBN 0 521 37178 3 hardback
ISBN 0 521 37815 X paperback

Contents

Notes on the contributors

Tamás Bauer is senior research fellow at the Institute of Economics of the Hungarian Academy of Sciences and professor of economics at the University of Frankfurt, Germany. He published a book on investment cycles in centrally planned economies in 1981 and has written numerous articles on economic reforms and economic policies in the countries of Eastern Europe. He is currently working on an analysis of the recent developments in Soviet and East European economic systems.

G. A. Cohen is Chichele Professor of Social and Political Theory at the University of Oxford and a fellow of All Souls. His publications include *Karl Marx's Theory of History: A Defence* (Oxford University Press, 1978) and *History, Labour and Freedom: Themes from Marx* (Oxford University Press, 1988). His contribution to the present volume is part of his current work on freedom and justice in relation to the conflict between capitalism and socialism.

Jon Elster is professor of political science at the University of Chicago and research director at the Institute for Social Research, Oslo. His publications include *Making Sense of Marx* (Cambridge University Press, 1985); *Sour Grapes* (Cambridge University Press, 1983); *Explaining Technical Change* (Cambridge University Press, 1983); *Ulysses and the Sirens* (Cambridge University Press, 1979, rev. ed. 1984); and *Logic and Society* (Wiley, 1978). He is currently working on problems related to bargaining, collective action and social justice.

Karl Ove Moene is professor of economics at the University of Oslo. His international publications include articles on unemployment problems, investments under uncertainty, bureaucratic interaction and collective wage bargaining. He is currently working on problems related to unemployment and income determination in economic systems with different ownership structures.

Alec Nove is professor emeritus, University of Glasgow, Scotland, and formerly director of the Institute of Soviet and East European Studies at that university. He is the author of *An Economic History of the USSR, The Soviet Economic System, Economics of Feasible Socialism,* and *Stalinism and After* and has just completed a book with the tentative title *Glasnost in Action.*

John E. Roemer is professor of economics and director of the Program in Economy, Justice, and Society at the University of California at Davis. His books include *A General Theory of Exploitation and Class* (Harvard University Press, 1982) and *Free to Lose: An Introduction to Marxist Economic Philosophy* (Harvard University Press, 1988). Current research interests include axiomatic modelling of theories of justice and the decentralisability of resource allocation in economies with public ownership.

György Sziráczki is a lecturer at the Karl Marx University of Economics, Budapest, and a member of Girton College, Cambridge. He is the coeditor of *Labour Market and Second Economy in Hungary* (Campus, 1985). He is currently working on problems related to work organisation, labour market and industrial relations.

Martin L. Weitzman is professor of economics at the Massachusetts Institute of Technology. He is a fellow of the Econometric Society and a member of the American Academy of Arts and Sciences. He has written numerous technical articles, and his book, *The Share Economy,* was translated into seven languages. His specialty is comparative economic systems, and he is currently working on problems related to profit sharing, productivity and worker participation.

1 Introduction

Jon Elster and Karl Ove Moene

The essays collected in this volume are based on a common concern. Capitalism – actually existing capitalism – appears in many respects to be an ugly, irrational, wasteful way of organising the production and distribution of goods and services. Mass unemployment as is currently observed is most advanced capitalist economies is the most striking form of this waste. Yet today we cannot say as confidently as many socialists have in the past that it is easy to create a better system. Indeed, many would say that the question whether a better system is feasible remains unresolved. The main cause of the disenchantment of socialists is the deplorable record of central planning, which in the socialist tradition was always the panacea for the ills of capitalism. Even with respect to full employment, which is often cited as the main and, for some, decisive advantage of Soviet-type economies, the performance of centrally planned economics is less than brilliant. Full employment is more or less achieved, but labour is heavily underutilised.[1] In other important respects centrally planned economies tend to do very badly. The ugliness of capitalism makes us look to central planning for a possible remedy, but the irrationality of central planning sends us back to capitalism as, probably, the lesser evil.[2]

Five of the essays in the present volume discuss whether there could be alternatives to presently existing capitalism other than central plan-

We are indebted to our colleagues in the Work and Social Justice project at the Institute for Social Research in Oslo for valuable discussions of an earlier draft of this chapter and to the Norwegian Social Science Research Council for financial support.

[1]See J. L. Porket, 'Unemployment in the Midst of Labour Waste', *Survey* 29 (1985): 19–28; J. Adam, *Employment and Wage Policies in Poland, Czechoslovakia and Hungary since 1950* (London: Macmillan Press, 1984); J. Kornai, *The Economics of Shortage* (Amsterdam: North-Holland, 1980). There are signs that in the Soviet Union full employment is beginning to be seen as an obstacle to economic modernisation.

[2]This is a main theme in J. Dunn, *The Politics of Socialism* (Cambridge University Press, 1984).

ning.[3] Could, for instance, central planning be tempered by the market, or capitalism tempered by planning? In their contributions Tamás Bauer and György Sziráczki consider the former alternative. Bauer argues that the market cannot achieve the aim of offering correct signals to economic agents unless the economy as a whole is organised on a decentralised, competitive basis; otherwise the signals are distorted and unclear. He also mentions a phenomenon more fully discussed by Sziráczki: the emergence of independent work partnerships in Hungarian industry. Although such inside subcontracting is likely to increase the flexibility of the firms that employ it, the fact that it is embedded within a bureaucratic framework makes it unlikely that a fully competitive system will be achieved. Alec Nove explains why any market economy, capitalist or otherwise, must be supplemented by some elements of central planning, although he does not argue that capitalism with this supplement is the solution to all problems created by pure laissez-faire capitalism. Martin Weitzman suggests reform of capitalist firms as the remedy for unemployment. If management and labour could be led to bargain over their respective shares in the net product rather than over the wage rate, firms would have an incentive to hire all available labour. A more radical alternative is worker ownership or control of firms, within the general framework of a market economy. Some properties of such firms are explored by Karl Ove Moene, who gives special emphasis to the comparison between labour cooperatives and capitalist firms with strong unions.

From economic theory and the historical experience we can learn something about the expected properties of alternative systems. It remains, however, to evaluate them. Three of the contributors to this volume discuss criteria that could enter into a comparative evaluation. In the spirit of social choice theory and bargaining theory, John Roemer defines a number of conditions one would want to impose on acceptable mechanisms for income distribution and discusses whether they can be satisfied simultaneously. G. A. Cohen asks whether private ownership of one's own skills and talents is compatible with equality of condition, both of these being prima facie desirable goals. Jon Elster proposes a definition of self-realisation and discusses the conditions under which it could become more widespread than it is presently.

A central theme of several of the essays is that any acceptable alterna-

---

[3]Note that we do not discuss 'pure' capitalism, free of monopolies, cartels and state interventions, as an alternative to actually existing capitalism. For reasons too obvious and too numerous to mention, we do not believe that this ideal system, if somehow introduced by fiat, would survive for an instant.

tive to present-day capitalism will have to rely on the market.[4] To discuss the methodological and substantive questions involved, it is convenient to focus on the more radical alternative: market socialism, based on workers' ownership of the means of production. Codetermination and profit sharing are less radical departures from the present system, since they take as given not only the market system but also private ownership of the means of production.[5] They differ from presently existing capitalism mainly in the modalities of wage- and work-related decision making, leaving the crucial decisions about employment, product mixes, prices, investment and closedowns in the hands of the owners. If Martin Weitzman is right, reforms of this less radical kind could have a massive impact on employment. Yet in the traditional debate over capitalism, employment is not the only or even the main value at stake. To survey the wider range or criteria, a more radical alternative for comparison is useful.

We shall proceed as follows. In Section 1.1 we discuss some of the main normative criteria that are relevant to a comparison of different economic systems. These include static efficiency (including full employment), dynamic efficiency, self-realisation, participation, community, quality of preferences, stability, economic freedom and income distribution. In Section 1.2 we discuss some general methodological issues that arise in a comparison of economic systems, with emphasis on the comparison of capitalism with market socialism. The central problem in this section is the difficulty of inferring the global, long-run, steady-state properties of a system from knowledge about its performance in the short run and on a small scale. In Section 1.3 we discuss some arguments concerning the performance of market socialism along some normative dimensions. Here we also include a brief discussion of the role of labour unions in an economy of labour cooperatives.

---

[4]Mention should be made of a third mode of economic organisation, distinct from both the market and central planning. K. Polanyi has argued (*The Great Transformation* [Boston: Beacon Press, 1957]) that *reciprocity* – giving and receiving according to need – has been the dominant mode of exchange in many traditional societies. S.-C. Kolm (*La bonne economie* [Paris: Presses Universitaires de France, 1984]) argues that it could and should also be made the dominant principle for complex industrial economies. In the absence of a sketch of the institutions that would embody the principle, the argument remains utopian.

[5]Codetermination has been implemented mainly in West Germany. A general discussion is R. A. McCain, 'Empirical Implications of Worker Participation in Management', in D. C. Jones and S. Svejnar (eds.), *Participatory and Self-Managed Firms: Evaluating Economic Performances* (Lexington, Mass.: Lexington Books, 1982), pp. 17–44. A study of the German case is J. Svejnar, 'Codetermination and Productivity: Empirical Evidence from the Federal Republic of Germany', ibid., pp. 199–212.

4   *Jon Elster and Karl Ove Moene*

1.1 Criteria of evaluation

The criteria to be discussed in this section are relatively uncontroversial, in the sense that almost everybody would agree that, other things being equal, it is better if they are satisfied than if they are not. It would, however, be an impossibly stringent requirement to demand of an alternative to capitalism that it be superior on some dimensions and inferior on none.[6] One must expect that any alternative will be superior in some respects and inferior in others. The overall assessment and comparison must then rest on a general theory of social justice that allows us to stipulate the trade-offs involved. We do not here attempt to offer any such theory, but our opinions – we do not claim they are more than that – may occasionally come through.

1.1.1 Information and trust

The comparative study of economic systems usually centers on the notion of efficiency. At the most general level, the problem is that of economising on information and trust. Central planning would be a perfect system, superior to any market economy, if these two resources were available in unlimited quantities.[7] With full information about all relevant economic constraints and possibilities, a centrally planned economy could allocate resources in a way that took full account of the externalities that underlie many of the failures of the market system. With full trust between principal and agents, the centrally decided allocation would be carried out without any waste or distortions due to self-interest or opportunism. Both assumptions are dangerously fragile. The kind of information required for a well-functioning planned economy is probably unavailable in principle.[8] In contrast, trust among economic agents is not necessarily impossible in principle. Indeed, some amount of trust must be present in any complex economic system, and it is far from inconceivable that systems with a higher general level of trust could evolve. It would be risky, however, to make higher levels of trust a cor-

[6]Dunn, *Politics of Socialism*, p. 34, asserts nevertheless that 'to claim . . . a right to rule with justification, a socialist party would need ideally to possess an understanding of the society as it is which showed socialist policies to be a necessary remedy for, or at least a beneficial alleviation of, some of its major existing demerits and to threaten none of its existing merits'.

[7]Actually, this is a simplification. Central planning unencumbered by the problems of information and trust would still run into the problem of consistent preference aggregation.

[8]Even were it available, the economic agents in a centrally planned economy often have an incentive to provide incorrect information. The problems of trust and information overlap.

nerstone of economic reform. We may hope that trust will come about as a by-product of a good economic system (and thus make the system even better), but one would be putting the cart before the horse were one to bank on trust, solidarity and altruism as the preconditions for reform.[9] In what follows, this necessity to economise on information and trust is taken for granted.

1.1.2 Efficiency
There can be trade-offs between different efficiency criteria. A system that maximises static efficiency – the optimal use and allocation of existing resources – does not in general maximise dynamic efficiency – the optimal creation of new resources.[10] Contrary to some statements of Marx's theory of history, it does not make unambiguous sense to say that property rights systems rise and fall according to their tendency to promote 'the use and development' of the productive forces, since a system that is optimal with respect to use need not be optimal with respect to development. Two well-known examples of the trade-off between static and dynamic efficiency are the patent system and the role of the entrepreneur. The paradox of the patent system is that by slowing down the diffusion of knowledge it ensures that there is more knowledge to diffuse.[11] The paradox of the entrepreneur stems from his identification with the firm (his role as the 'residual claimant'). On the one hand, the intensity of his search for new methods and markets will be greater than that of a salaried manager; on the other hand, his criteria for accepting or rejecting the outcome of the search will be inefficient, because of his risk aversion.[12] In principle, and speaking very crudely, one would expect that in the long run a dynamically superior system will outperform one that is statically more efficient. At the same time, if gains in static efficiency can be realised quickly, they may have greater political efficacy than long-term prospects.

Unemployment is a form of static inefficiency. So is underemployment, that is, the inefficient use and allocation of labour. (We may also refer to this as overemployment, since it usually implies that too many workers are employed.) In capitalist economies the workers who actu-

---

[9]For a discussion of some reasons that trust cannot be brought about by intentional planning, see G. Hawthorn, 'Trust and Innovation', in D. Gambetta (ed.), *Trust and Agency* (Oxford: Blackwell Publisher, forthcoming).

[10]A well-known statement of the distinction is that of J. Schumpeter, *Capitalism, Socialism and Democracy* (London: Allen & Unwin, 1961), p. 83.

[11]Joan Robinson, *The Accumulation of Capital* (London: Macmillan Press 1956), p. 87.

[12]K. Arrow, *Essays in the Theory of Risk-Bearing* (Amsterdam: North-Holland, 1971), p. 149.

ally have a job tend to be efficiently employed, in the sense that their wage equals the value of their marginal product. In centrally planned economies all workers are employed, but the value of their marginal product may fall far short of the wage. The rationale behind this practice is that 'it is more efficient to let people work – even if their contribution is below labour costs – than to support them.[13] It might indeed be better, ceteris paribus, for people to be working inefficiently than not working at all, but the incentive effects on workers and enterprises ensure that other things will not be equal.

Consider in particular the following argument that modern societies are condemned to choose between unemployment and underemployment. One form of the latter is shirking, that is, workers' not putting in the work effort they have contracted to. Under full employment workers have no incentive to avoid shirking, since if they are caught and fired they can easily find a job elsewhere. It follows that

> to induce its workers not to shirk, the firm attempts to pay more than the going wage; then, if a worker is caught shirking and is fired, he will pay a penalty. If it pays one firm to raise its wage, however, it will pay all firms to raise their wages. When they all raise their wages, the incentive not to shirk again disappears. But as all firms raise their wages, their demand for labor decreases, and unemployment results. With unemployment, even if all firms pay the same wages, a worker has an incentive not to shirk. For, if he is fired, an individual will not immediately obtain another job. The equilibrium unemployment rate must be sufficiently high that it pays workers to work rather than to take the risk of being caught shirking.[14]

Hence in the capitalist wage system, external inefficiency is a condition for internal efficiency.

This argument is modified by the existence of cost to the worker of leaving one job for another. A change of job may involve a change of residence, with all the concomitant economic and psychological costs. Moreover, by involving the breakup of firm-specific friendships, it imposes costs similar to those of divorce.[15] Nevertheless, there are probably many workers who are not deterred from shirking by such ties to the firm. Since the firm cannot know who will and who will not be deterred by the risk of being caught and fired, it may well decide to assume

[13]Adam, *Employment and Wage Policies*, p. 8.

[14]C. Shapiro and J. Stiglitz, 'Equilibrium Unemployment as a Worker Discipline Device', *American Economic Review* 74 (1984): 443–4, at p. 433.

[15]It is also true that the argument takes no account of firm-specific skills, which may prevent workers from getting equally well paid jobs elsewhere. Yet such skills also make workers more valuable to the firm than their potential replacements would be. The net effect of these two opposing tendencies is in general indeterminate.

that any worker will shirk if he has an equally good job open to him else-where. To transcend this dismal choice between sluggish full employment and dynamic unemployment one would have to create a system in which workers had an incentive not to shirk.

1.1.3 Alienation and self-realisation

The notion of efficiency can be taken in a narrow sense, in which labour is considered solely as an input to the production process with a constant disutility to the worker. It can also, however, be taken in an extended sense that allows for 'producers' preferences' over different ways of organising the production process.[16] The two central work-related values that might enter into these preferences are self-realisation and participation. Neither capitalism nor central planning offers much scope for participation. By and large, they rest on a firmly hierarchical basis. They are not systematically inimical to self-realisation in the work process, nor do they systematically favour it. If workers achieve self-realisation in hierarchically organised enterprises, it will largely be an accident. Capitalism is somewhat superior to central planning in this respect, because of its reliance on the market mechanism. If workers have a real desire (as distinct from a mere verbal wish) for work that offers scope for self-realisation, they are presumably willing to take a cut in wages to achieve it. If the loss of efficiency implied by switching to techniques with more scope for self-realisation is not too large, an entrepreneur might make a profit doing so. Yet the self-realisation thus achieved would be precarious. It would be a means to profit maximisation, not an end in itself that could guide the search for new techniques and organisational principles.

Alienation, in the socialist tradition, means several things. It can mean absence of self-realisation, that is, the performance of routine work that is monotonous and unrewarding. It can also mean, however, the absence of communitarian feelings and values. In this sense, alienation has traditionally been linked to the horizontal division between firms in capitalism, not to the vertical division within firms. The arms-length character of market transactions, with the built-in incentives for cheating, deceiving and misrepresenting, subvert the possibility of real community. Personal relations become superficial and ephemeral. A closely related criticism of market economies, capitalist or otherwise, is that they

---

[16]On this notion see U. Pagano, *Work and Welfare in Economic Theory* (Oxford: Blackwell Publisher, 1985), and A. Nove, *The Economics of Feasible Socialism* (London: Allen & Unwin, 1983), p. 199.

generate desires for objects that are inherently worthless. The capacity for the efficient production of junk cannot be a strong argument for market organisation, when the desire for these products is itself a product of the economic system.

The more general problem is the following: Given that preferences are shaped largely by the social environment, how can they also serve to justify existing social arrangements?[17] If people in a market economy like the kinds of relationships and goods that market economies tend to produce, and people in a communally organised economy have a similarly endogenous preference for their society, one might conclude that there is no reason to change or to prefer the status quo, except on the basis of arguments derived from costs of transition, which will always favour the status quo. One way out of this relativistic dilemma would be to appeal to interpersonally comparable preferences, assuming such comparisons to be at least roughly possible. Even if workers in capitalism prefer capitalism and workers in socialism prefer socialism, one might prefer the society with the greatest sum total of utility.

Yet this cannot be the whole story. Even if it turned out that slaves in a slave society were happier than workers in a capitalist society, we would hesitate to assert a preference for slavery. We might, however, be marginally more willing to do so if slaves in some meaningful sense had the option of not becoming slaves. If X is preferred to Y in the presence of Y as a feasible alternative, the preference has greater weight than it does if X is preferred to Y and the latter is not a feasible option. In the case of slavery, this remark might seem besides the point. What matters here is to block the option of voluntary and irreversible lifelong enslavement, not to open the option of freedom. Yet when decisions are reversible, the principle that preferences should be respected when there is genuine freedom of choice seems compelling. If workers in a centrally planned economy had the unobstructed option of setting up capitalist firms and nevertheless did not use it, we would have more confidence in their preference for central planning than if such ventures were illegal or very costly. (Moreover, one might ask whether unemployed workers under capitalism are voluntarily unemployed if they dislike and therefore dismiss central planning as a way of achieving full employment).[18]

Individual workers in a capitalist economy do not, however, have the option of setting up a centrally planned economy. A little capitalism is a

---

[17]See also J. Elster, *Sour Grapes* (Cambridge University Press, 1983), chap. 3.
[18]On this question see T. Haavelmo, 'On the Notion of Involuntary Economic Decisions', *Econometrica 18* (1950): 1–8.

meaningful notion; a little central planning is not. Another, more subtle problem arises if one compares two decentralised systems – that is, systems that can be implemented at the level of individual enterprises, such as wage capitalism versus profit-sharing capitalism or capitalism versus market socialism. Here the problem of stability becomes crucial.

1.1.4 Externalities

In the presence of externalities, individual preferences can be a bad guide to social choice. Even if mode A of economic organisation is collectively superior to mode B, in the sense that all individuals would be better off if all worked in enterprises organised along the lines of A than if all were organised in B-type firms, workers in an individual enterprise might not find it in their interest to take the first step from an all-B system towards an all-A system and, in addition, might find it in their interest to take the first step from A to B. If the externalities have the first of these effects but not the second, we are in the presence of an Assurance Game: Both the inferior and the superior system are stable. If they have both effects, the situation is that of a Prisoner's Dilemma: Only the inferior system is stable.[19] We return to the question of externalities in market socialism. For externalities of profit sharing we refer to Chapter 3, by Weitzman.

If the inferior system is stable, one might want to legislate in favour of the superior alternative, by forbidding or taxing the inferior mode of organising firms. Other things being equal, this interference in economic freedom is undesirable. State intervention is costly to maintain and, very importantly, detracts from the untrammelled freedom of action that is a central component of individual autonomy. Even people who do not want to *use* their freedom to do certain things might nevertheless want to *have* it, if only to ensure that their desire not to use it is not due to its absence.[20] If the situation has the structure of an Assurance Game, legislation could, however, be a temporary measure. After a while, one might reintroduce the freedom to create type B enterprises. If the situation has the form of a Prisoner's Dilemma, permanent legislation would be required.

---

[19] On these concepts and an application to the present type of problem, see D. Miller, 'Market Neutrality and the failure of Co-operatives', *British Journal of Political Science 11* (1981): 309–29.
[20] Elster, *Sour Grapes*, p. 128.

1.1.5 Conflicting preferences

More difficult problems arise if one assumes, more realistically, that one system is preferred by most but not all people. Assume that a majority of the workers prefers an all-A system over an all-B system, whereas the minority has the opposite preference. We also assume, as before, that nobody wants to make the first move away from an all-B system. A pertinent question is whether the majority would prefer a mixed system in which they worked in A-type enterprises and the minority in B-type enterprises over an all-B economy. Assume, for specificity, that 70 percent prefer an all-A system and 30 percent prefer an all-B system. There are several possibilities:

1.   The members of the majority prefer a system in which 70 percent work in A-type firms and 30 percent in B-type firms over the all-B system. This amounts to saying that the A sector is collectively stable.

1.1.   It might also be individually stable, in the sense that once it has reached 70 percent no members of the majority are tempted to defect. In this case temporary subsidies rather than temporary or permanent legislation would be appropriate.

1.2.   If the A sector is individually unstable, a universal ban on B-type firms might still be unnecessary. If the members of the majority could somehow impose on themselves a ban on working for B-type firms, they would not have to force their will on the minority.

1.2.1. The assumption that members of the majority would defect from the A sector is consistent with the notion that in an all-A economy no members of the majority would be tempted to defect. The presence of the minority would nevertheless, in the absence of legislation, make the situation unravel: The minority would defect and thereby create an incentive for the majority to defect.

1.2.2. The assumption is also consistent with the opposite notion, that B-type firms are always individually preferred, regardless of the number of A-type firms in the economy.

2.   Finally, the majority might not prefer a mixed economy over the all-B economy. In that case it would have to force its will on the minority to eliminate the externalities. It might do that in case 1.2 as well, since in that situation members of the majority would, in the absence of universal legislation, have an incentive

to present themselves as members of the minority. It might want to do so even if there were no incentive problem, since the majority would always be even better off in the absence of the minority.

Two ceteris paribus propositions seem plausible. First, state interference with economic freedom is more acceptable the larger the number of individuals affected by the negative externalities. In particular, intervention is more acceptable if it benefits everyone than it is if it amounts to the imposition of the will of a majority on a minority. Second, the imposition of the will of a minority is more acceptable if the majority is not collectively self-sustaining than if it is. For the majority to ban the organisational form preferred by the minority in order to eliminate the opportunity for members of the majority to represent themselves, falsely, as members of the minority, would be to let the minority pay the cost of solving the collective-action problem of the majority.

1.1.6 Some broader issues

Is anyone who accepts the arguments for political democracy compelled, by the same logic, to embrace economic democracy and workers' ownership of their enterprises?[21] Is economic democracy a condition for political democracy? More specifically, is economic democracy necessary for the economic equality that is needed for a functioning political democracy?[22] Or perhaps because it fosters the spirit of participation?[23] Or is it rather the other way around, so that economic freedom, including the freedom to set up capitalist firms, is a necessary condition for political democracy?[24] Or should one limit oneself to the weaker conclusion, that a decentralised economic system – whether it is based on private or cooperative ownership – is a condition for political democracy? Is the consumer's sovereignty a condition for the citizen's sovereignty? We tend to think that the logical and sociological connections between the economic and the political realms are somewhat less tight than these questions would suggest. Limitations of space prevent us, however, from going more deeply into these issues.

[21]R. Dahl, *A Preface to Economic Democracy* (New Haven, Conn.: Yale University Press, 1985); M. Walzer, *Spheres of Justice* (New York: Basic, 1983) p. 291–303.

[22]R. Krouse and M. McPherson, 'On Rawlsian Justice in Political Economy: Capitalism, "Property-Owning Democracy", and the Welfare State', in A. Guttman (ed.), *Democracy and the Welfare State* (Princeton, N.J.: Princeton University Press, 1988), pp. 79–105.

[23]C. Pateman, *Participation and Democratic Theory* (Cambridge University Press, 1970).

[24]A classic version of this argument is M. Friedman, *Capitalism and Freedom* (University of Chicago Press, 1962).

Finally, different economic systems tend to be associated with different profiles of income distribution. Ceteris paribus, a system that generates the more equal distribution is to be preferred. For market economies, one may distinguish between the distribution that would be observed in the absence of redistributive political measures and what would be observed with redistribution constrained by some concern for efficiency and economic freedom.[25] With central planning the distinction does not apply, since the desired distribution of income can be realised directly. Next to the absence of overt unemployment, relatively equal distribution of income is usually seen as the major advantage of centrally planned economies. It is not clear, however, that the argument is valid, since what matters in a *Nomenklatura* society is not so much income as the availability of goods to spend one's income on.

1.2 The methodology of institutional comparison

How can we find out what market socialism might be like? There are two possible sources: theory and experience. There is a good deal of economic theory dealing with the behaviour of labour cooperatives in partial and general equilibrium. There is empirical evidence about the performance of isolated cooperatives, about one large group of cooperatives (Mondragon and the Israeli kibbutzim) within an otherwise capitalist economy and about one economy (Yugoslavia) based largely on the principle of workers' self-management.[26]

The economic theory of cooperatives, in its present state, is not sufficiently developed to offer robust conclusions about the long-term, large-

[25]Two well-known forms of the efficiency constraint are the following: First, one could allow redistribution as long as it adds to the sum total of utility, even if it detracts from the sum total of wealth produced. Second, one could allow redistribution as long as it benefits the worst-off group in society.

The economic-freedom constraint need not be the extreme libertarian form that any redistributive taxation is an unacceptable interference with freedom. One might argue, for instance, that lump-sum taxation, which in principle is the most efficient form of redistribution, is unacceptable on grounds of liberty because it removes the decision about how much to work from the free choice of the individual.

[26]We will not draw heavily on the Israeli experience, since the kibbutzim, even more than other cooperatives, are heavily dependent on exceptionally strong ideological motivations.

Nor will we draw heavily on the Yugoslav experience, because of its special features. These include the relatively underdeveloped character of the Yugoslav economy, the strong regional conflicts in Yugoslavia and the varying but never negligible role of the Communist Party. On these features and the methodological problems arising from them see S. Estrin, *Self-Management: Economic Theory and Yugoslav Practice* (Cambridge University Press, 1983), chap. 3.

scale viability of cooperatives. Most theoretical studies of cooperatives treat the firm as a black box that differs from its capitalist counterpart only in maximising net revenue per worker rather than the rate of return on capital. By assuming that cooperatives and capitalist firms operate along the same production function, they neglect the crucial issue of now workers' control and ownership affect work incentives, productivity and the capacity for innovation.[27] In general, the mainstream theoretical comparison between labour management and its capitalist twin is done in a very stylised manner, with several unfortunate consequences.

First, in discussions of efficiency issues the idealised capitalist firm is assumed to operate with full centralised control of management. Effects of conflicts of interest between workers and employers, or between management and owners, are largely neglected. Labour inputs are treated just as any other factor of production, on a par with raw materials and energy. In this theoretical setup, the cooperative cannot perform better than its capitalist twin. As long as the cooperative is assumed to maximise net revenue per worker and to operate in an environment without credit rationing, it will hire fewer members and choose excessively capital-intensive technology compared with its capitalist counterpart. A more interesting comparison would take account of the facts that workers have some influence on the behaviour of the capitalist firm, through their local unions, and that external ownership is separated from managerial control of the firm. Under these more realistic assumptions, the introduction of self-management could reduce both types of conflict of interest.

Second, the comparison between the two types of organisation is usually carried out within a general-equilibrium framework, in which all markets are assumed to clear in every period. More insight, however, would be gained by comparing the behavior of the twins in situations with market disequilibria of various sorts. We would then ask whether labour-managed firms are equally as inclined as capitalist firms to generate environments with sales constraints and unemployment. We might further ask how external shocks to the economy are propagated through

---

[27]Important exceptions are the recent 'property rights' and 'transaction costs' approaches, which do not treat the production function as independent of the institutional arrangement. See, for instance, M. C. Jensen and W. H. Meckling, 'Rights and Production Functions: An Application to Labor-Determined Firms and Codetermination', *Journal of Business* 52 (1979): 469–506, and O. Williamson, *The Economic Institutions of Capitalism* (New York: the Free Press, 1985). These approaches yield mainly qualitative conclusions, however. Until more fully specified models are available, it is hard to judge the importance of the effects they predict. See also the discussion of work incentives, risk aversion and innovation in Section 1.3.

firms with different organisation structures. The effects of shock might be mainly nominal or they could be mainly real quantity effects, depending inter alia on the propensity of firms to lay off workers in a depressed state of the product market.

Third, in modern capitalist societies there is a tendency to replace market-oriented decision making by bargaining at different levels, especially between interest organisations created by the present ownership structure. The government also takes part in the bargaining process, not only as an arbitrator, but increasingly also as an active player, by linking changes in taxes and social security to the agreements reached by the interest organisations. One consequence is the devolution of power from the parliament to the organisations. 'Formally, the Parliament is, of course, free to reject the State Budget implications of the agreements reached in bargaining, but in practice this is a very difficult decision to take when the whole functioning of the economic system is dependent upon the agreement. The Parliament therefore loses some of its power over such matters'.[28] A transition from wage capitalism to a system of labour-managed firms might eliminate some important social conflicts and reduce the need for bargaining in which the government takes part. This could improve the functioning of democracy, by increasing the power of parliament and by reducing the informal constraints on economic policy making.

We do not deny, of course, that the mainstream economic theory of self-management is a useful, indeed indispensable, tool for exploring the properties of labour cooperatives. We believe, however, that economic theory in its present state is most useful for questions of fine-tuning. It directs itself to choices within systems, not to the choice of a system. To discuss the latter, more fundamental issue we must consider empirical evidence about the actual performance of the alternatives. We then face the methodological problem of how to infer the large-scale, long-term, steady-state properties of a system from small-scale, short-term evidence.

To discuss this problem, we shall use a framework derived from Tocqueville's discussion of political democracy in America.[29] His argument, addressed mainly to French sceptics about democracy, took the form of refuting a series of fallacies, four altogether. Seeing why these

---

[28]L. Johansen, 'The Bargaining Society and the Inefficiency of Bargaining', *Kyklos* 32 (1979): 497–522, at p. 505.

[29]For a fuller discussion see J. Elster, 'Consequences of Constitutional Choice: Reflections on Tocqueville', in J. Elster and R. Slagstad (eds.), *Constitutionalism and Democracy* (Cambridge University Press, 1988), pp. 81–102.

fallacies are indeed fallacies helps us understand important features of social causality. We shall argue that it also helps us understand and avoid some of the methodological pitfalls in the study of economic democracy.

1.2.1 Local versus global effects

Tocqueville provides an instructive example of the fallacious tendency to generalise from the effect of an institutional change when implemented on a small scale to its effect when carried out on a large scale. Discussing the effects of marrying for love, a widespread practice in democracies, he writes that 'our ancestors conceived a singular opinion with regard to marriage. As they had noticed that the few love matches which took place in their days almost always ended in tragedy, they came to the firm conclusion that in such matters it was very dangerous to rely on one's own heart'.[30] He goes on to point out two reasons for considering this view to be untenable. The first is negative discrimination: To marry for love in a society in which this is the exception is to court disaster, since going against the current tends to create hostility in others and, in turn, bitterness in oneself. The second is adverse self-selection: Only very opinionated individuals will go against the current in the first place – and this is not a characteristic that is conducive to happy marriages.

The performance of labour cooperatives may similarly be influenced by (positive or negative) discrimination and by (positive or negative) self-selection. Consider first positive discrimination. It has been argued that, to survive in a capitalist economy, cooperatives need an ideologically motivated support organisation.[31] To the extent that such organisations are in place, the good performance of the cooperatives supported by them obviously does not allow us to infer that a system of cooperatives would perform equally well. Negative discrimination has been more widely discussed. It has frequently been alleged that the capitalist environment, and in particular the financial institutions of capitalism, discriminates against cooperatives, so that the bad performance of isolated cooperatives must not be allowed to count as an argument against the cooperative principle.[32] Against this it has been said, first, that in a competitive financial market no institution can afford to pass up a profitable

---

[30]*Democracy in America* (New York: Anchor Books, 1969), p. 596.

[31]C. E. Gunn, *Workers' Self-Management in the United States* (Ithaca, N.Y.: Cornell University Press, 1984), pp. 57–61.

[32]See, for instance, S. Bowles and H. Gintis, *Schooling in Capitalist America* (New York: Basic, 1976), p. 62.

opportunity[33] and, second, that of investment and lending.[34] The objection neglects, however, the fact that local competitors of the cooperative might well have an incentive to undersell it.[35]

Positive self-selection can occur if the few cooperatives in an otherwise capitalist environment attract (or admit only) highly motivated and idealistic individuals who are willing to work hard, to suffer the time costs of participation and if necessary to take a wage cut. The forest workers' cooperatives in the northwestern part of the United States seem to correspond to this description.[36] Similarly, the Mondragon cooperatives in Spain have been able to screen applicants and to admit only those with cooperative value systems.[37] To an even higher degree, positive self-selection occurs in the Israeli kibbutzim.[38] Clearly, the viability of such firms does not imply that the model could be easily transferred elsewhere. The situation is somewhat analogous to that of private, ideologically motivated schools versus municipal schools. Since the former are often able to attract exceptionally motivated teachers, they produce results that one could never expect to duplicate in a larger system in which teachers form a more or less average cross section of the population as a whole. Adverse self-selection could also occur, as in Tocqueville's example. 'These reform experiments might attract unstable individuals, excessive risktakers, and people lacking in pragmatic orientation'.[39]

The divergence of local and global effects can also arise without selection and discrimination, namely, if a positive or negative externality is operating. If an isolated cooperative can take a free ride on capitalist

[33]R. Nozick, *Anarchy, State and Utopia* (New York: Basic, 1974), pp. 252–3.
[34]Miller, 'Market Neutrality'. See also the discussion in Section 1.3.
[35]The following passage from a letter by John Stuart Mill illustrates the point: 'I beg to enclose a subscription of £10 to aid, as far as such a sum can do it, in the struggle which the co-operative platelock makers of Wolverhampton are sustaining against unfair competition on the part of the masters in the trade. Against fair competition I have no desire to shield them, . . . but to carry on business at a loss, in order to ruin competitors, is not fair competition. In such a contest, if prolonged, the competitors who have the smallest means, though they may have every other element of success, must necessarily be crushed through no fault of their own. . . . I am now convinced that they ought to be supported against the attempt to ruin them' (cited after Benjamin Jones, *Co-Operative Production* [London, 1894; reprint New York: Kelley, 1968], p. 438).
[36]Gunn, *Workers' Self-Management*, chap. 3.
[37]K. Bradley and A. Gelb, 'The Mondragon Cooperatives: Guidelines for a Cooperative Economy?' in Jones and Svejnar (eds.), *Participatory and Self-Managed Firms*, pp. 153–72.
[38]See A. Ben-Ner and E. Neuberger, 'Israel: The Kibbutz', in F. Stephen (ed.), *The Performance of Labour-Managed Firms* (New York: St. Martin's, 1982), pp. 186–213.
[39]L. Putterman, 'Some Behavioral Perspectives on the Dominance of Hierarchical over Democratic Forms of Enterprise', *Journal of Economic Behavior and Organization* 3 (1982): 139–60, at p. 152.

enterprises, it will perform better than it would do as part of a cooperative system. If cooperatives are bad at innovating but good at imitating, they can do well as they long as there are some dynamic capitalist firms they can imitate. More speculatively, the motivation to participate in self-managed firms could depend on a feeling of moral superiority which presupposes that most firms are capitalist.

Conversely, isolated cooperatives could be disadvantaged (a) by negative externalities created by capitalist firms or (b) by their failure to internalise positive externalities generated by themselves. An example of (a) would be the 'ideological externality' created by the presence of wage labour in the economy. In a largely capitalist environment, successful cooperatives will be tempted to employ some workers on a wage basis, to increase their ability to adjust flexibly to changes in market conditions. In so doing, however, they may end up losing both the intangible benefits from working in a democratic enterprise and any tangible productivity benefits that arise from the intangible ones. Another example of (a) is the 'collective bargaining externality' identified as follows by Peter Jay: 'Insofar as the crucial advantage urged for the labour-managed economy is that it would cause collective bargaining . . . to wither away, so dissolving the catastrophic dilemma of high unemployment or accelerating inflation, that cannot be tested by examining the experience of individual co-operatives in a capital-managed economy where the general need for trade union organization and collective bargaining is bound to be strongly felt'.[40]

An example of (b) would be the 'entrepreneurial externality' created by cooperatives. In a democratically run enterprise, entrepreneurially gifted individuals will not just make good decisions: They will also educate their fellow workers. The Mondragon workers, for instance, have their own technical school. If the workers who have benefitted from the education leave the firm and take a job in a capitalist enterprise, the education is in fact made available to other firms free of charge. Even if the cooperative is driven out of business because the private return to its activities is below that of the typical capitalist firm, the social return may be higher for the cooperative than for the capitalist firm. Another suggested example of (b) is the 'political externality' created by cooperatives. If members of cooperatives make better political citizens and if civic spirit is a public good, cooperatives generate diffuse benefits not

[40]P. Jay, 'The Workers' Cooperative Economy', in A. Clayre (ed.), *The Political Economy of Co-operation and Participation* (New York: Oxford University Press, 1980), pp. 9–45, at p. 40.

captured by the price mechanism.[41] Against this one may object, first, that for many people economic participation will reduce rather than enhance their participation in political affairs. Paraphrasing Oscar Wilde, there are only so many evenings to go around. Second, it is doubtful that participation in economic decision making will have these positive effects in other arenas unless it is regarded as valuable in its own right. The spillover effects of participation are essentially by-products.[42]

1.2.2 Partial versus net effects

An amusing example in Tocqueville is the following: 'As there is no pre-cautionary organization in the United States, there are more fires than in Europe, but generally they are put out more speedily, because the neigh-bors never fail to come quickly to the danger spot'.[43] The structure of the argument is the following: We want to examine the effect of an inde-pendent variable (political regime) on a dependent variable (the number of houses destroyed by fire). Between cause and effect there are two intermediate variables, which interact multiplicatively: the number of houses that catch fire and the proportion of fires that are not quickly extinguished. One can easily imagine adversaries of American democ-racy focussing on one of the partial effects and its advocates emphasising the other. The real issue, however, is whether the net effect is positive or negative. In the absence of more precise information about the strength of the opposing tendencies, it may not be possible to answer this question.

Similar causal structures can be expected to arise in the case of market socialism. Indeed, the dual character of that system is obvious, since *market* and *socialism* have quite different connotations and may be expected to lead in quite opposite directions. Thus the socialist aspect of the system – that is, the workers' ownership of their means of produc-tion – might be expected to promote a spirit of cooperation and solidar-ity, whereas the market aspect would tend to work in the direction of competitiveness and even hostility. It is hard to say *a priori* whether per-sonal relations in a market socialist society would be shaped mainly by the former or mainly by the latter.

The impact on the distribution of income is similarly ambiguous. On the one hand, one would expect the within-firm distribution of income

[41]Pateman, *Participation and Democratic Theory*; see also R. Krouse and M. McPherson, 'A "Mixed" Property Regime: Equality and Liberty in a Market Economy', *Ethics* 97 (1985): 119–38.
[42]For this notion see Elster, *Sour Grapes*, chap. 2, sec. 9.
[43]Tocqueville, *Democracy in America*, p. 723.

between workers of different skill levels to be relatively egalitarian. On the other hand, there could well be durable inequalities between workers of similar skills in different firms. Since there is no labour market in a market socialist economy, there is no natural tendency for wages to reach a uniform level. Successful firms, moreover, have no tendency to expand and thus to absorb other workers.[44] And even if they do invite other workers to join them, the latecomers might get a lower return on their equity than the pioneers, if they have to pay the market value for a share in the firm.[45] One might expect that in a very profitable line of activity the creation of new firms would achieve what expansion of existing firms does in capitalism. The problem, of course, is that to create a new firm and to overcome the initial difficulties requires a great deal of time and that in the meantime the activity may have become less profitable. In a changing environment, mechanisms of adjustment must work rapidly; otherwise the moving target may never be reached or even approached.

One can only speculate about the net effect of these opposing tendencies. If the income differences between managers and workers in a market socialist economy are smaller than under capitalism and the differences among workers in different firms are larger, the overall inequality of income distribution, measured by some suitable index, might be larger or it might be smaller. The income differences might, moreover, be considered unjust if they are mainly a result of luck rather than of skill. It might not be socially acceptable if workers doing the same jobs in the same firm or doing similar jobs in different firms receive different incomes simply because some of them happened to be in the right firm at the right time.

1.2.3 Short-term versus long-term effects

This distinction is a special case of the preceding one, but sufficiently important to be singled out for separate consideration. On this point, Tocqueville writes that 'in the long run government by democracy should increase the real forces of a society, but it cannot immediately assemble, at one point and at a given time, forces as great as those at the disposal of an aristocratic government or an absolute monarchy'.[46] This

---

[44]For a simple and lucid exposition of the reasons that labour cooperatives behave differently from capitalist firms in this respect see J. Meade, 'The Theory of Labour-Managed Firms and of Profit-Sharing', *Economic Journal* 82 (1972): 402–28.

[45]Ibid. This practice is followed in the plywood cooperatives in the United States (see Gunn, 'Workers' Self-Management'), but not, for instance, in the Mondragon cooperatives.

[46]Tocqueville, *Democracy in America*, p. 224

holds in particular for warfare: 'An aristocratic people which, fighting against a democracy, does not succeed in bringing it to ruin in the first campaign always runs a great risk of being defeated by it'.[47]

The Schumpeterian distinction between static and dynamic efficiency illustrates this point. The standard argument, discussed below, is that market socialism is inferior to capitalism in both of these respects, because of the lack of an entrepreneur who is also the residual claimant. Consider, however, the following argument: 'While *static economizing on scarce decision-making capabilities,* which characterizes hierarchical organizations, may be advantageous in the short run, this same characteristic may have an associated property of retarding such multiplication of capabilities as might be brought about by a more participatory system, and which might, in fact, prove widely beneficial'.[48] This is Tocqueville's argument for political democracy transferred to economic democracy.

Note that the point here is not that short-term sacrifices may be a necessary causal condition for long-term growth, as exemplified by the need for investment (short-term sacrifice of consumption) as a means of securing future increases in consumption. Rather it is that short-term inefficiency (and the concomitant loss of consumption) may be an inevitable by-product of the system with the best long-term performance. The short-term sacrifice is correlated with the long-term performance, but does not cause it.

1.2.4 Transitional versus steady-state effects

Tocqueville writes that 'one must be careful not to confuse the fact of equality with the revolution which succeeds in introducing it into the state of society and into the laws'.[49] The endogenous, steady-state products of democracy must not be confused with the temporary products of democratisation. The latter may be undesirable, and yet the former very desirable, as Tocqueville shows in a number of examples. Conversely, in his notes for the second volume on the French Revolution, Tocqueville argues against the view that politically unfree regimes are especially favourable to literary creation because they leave more time to individuals for their private pursuits. Rather, it is the transition from freedom to the absence of freedom that tends to stimulate the arts.[50] Once tyranny becomes entrenched, the creative spirit withers.

[47]Ibid., p. 658.
[48]Putterman, 'Behavioral Perspectives', p. 149. Italics in original.
[49]Tocqueville, *Democracy in America*, p. 688.
[50]Alexis de Tocqueville, *L'Ancien Régime et la révolution*, 2 vols. (Paris: Gallimard, 1953), 2:345–46.

The argument has very wide application. To evaluate an economic, social or political system one must not look at its performance immediately after it has been introduced but wait until its endogenous, steady-state properties have had time to emerge.[51] Whether the transitional system performs better or worse than the new steadystate, it will certainly differ from it in important respects. 'Hence, to compare the efficiency of a participatory institution having hierarchically-adapted members, with that of a hierarchical institution having such members, is likely to be a biased procedure, since the participatory institution composed of such personnel may not be a fully appropriate proxy for the appropriately endowed participatory organization that might evolve under more ideal conditions'.[52] Conversely, in a successfully organised cooperative economy there might be transitional gains to be realised from reversal to hierarchy, since for a while it might be possible to enjoy both the capabilities generated by the cooperatives and the efficient utilisation of them that is made possible by hierarchy.

The upshot of this discussion is not that it is impossible to draw any lessons from experience. Whether the problems of generalising from local, short-term and transitional consequences are so serious that no conclusions can be drawn has to be decided on a case-by-case basis. The point is rather that in learning from experience one has to proceed with caution. Both excessively optimistic and excessively pessimistic views on the viability of market socialism might appear to be warranted if one did not take account of the biases we have considered in this section.

1.3 Properties and problems of market socialism

Broad and general conclusions about the viability of market socialism can emerge only from experience, with suitable account taken of the various biases discussed in the preceding section. Yet experience can to some extent be guided by economic reasoning, which suggests that certain ways of organising self-management are more likely to work out than others. In this section we discuss some of the microeconomic and macroeconomic questions that have to be confronted by would-be founders of cooperatives and by political entrepreneurs. The issues include work

[51]Note that the distinction between transitional and steady-state effects does not coincide with that between short-term and long-term effects, since we may distinguish different temporal perspectives within the steady state.
[52]Putterman, 'Behavioral Perspectives', p. 149.

incentives, financial structure and the role of labour unions. Before we consider these questions, some definitional remarks on labour cooperatives and market socialism are required.

1.3.1 What is a cooperative?

The answer to the question might seem obvious: A cooperative is a firm in which the workers own the means of production and have full control over all economic decisions. Yet the answer, as it stands, is ambiguous and incomplete. It fails to capture the variety and complexity of existing cooperatives. We will not here propose a formal definition, but only point to some ways in which cooperatives can differ.

A basic problem is whether to define cooperatives in terms of ownership or in terms of control over decisions. These do not always go together. In Yugoslavia self-managing enterprises do not have full ownership of their means of production. In particular, they are legally forbidden to disinvest, that is, to sell capital goods or let the capital stock run down.[53] In a study of British cooperatives Derek Jones found that even in firms in which workers did not own a majority of the shares they had a majority on the governing board of the firm, because elections follow the principle 'One man, one vote' rather than 'one share, one vote'.[54] Jaroslav Vanek has argued that the optimal arrangement for a cooperative is to be financed fully by outside nonvoting equity capital, so that income accruing to workers would come to them qua workers and not qua capital owners.[55] Conversely, the formal conditions for worker ownership may be fulfilled without effective workers' control. In some of the American firms in which workers have gained a majority of the shares by employee stock ownership plans (ESOPS), the unequal distribution of shares among employees prevents the great majority of workers from having any effective influence on decisions.[56] (These firms follow the principle 'One share, one vote'.) Empirical studies of cooperatives and participation have explored both ownership and control as independent

---

[53]S. Sacks, *Self-Management and Efficiency: Large Corporations in Yugoslavia* (London: Allen & Unwin, 1983), p. 76.

[54]D. C. Jones, 'British Producer Cooperatives, 1948–1968: Productivity and Organizational Structure', in Jones and Svejnar (eds), *Participatory and Self-Managed Firms*, pp. 175–98, at p. 179.

[55]J. Vanek, 'The Basic Theory of Financing of Participatory Firms', in J. Vanek (ed.), *Self-Management* (Harmondsworth: Penguin Books, 1975), pp. 445–55. Vanek does not rule out workers' owning shares in their firms, but he does not require it either. If they hold shares, they are treated on a par with other shareholders.

[56]See Note, 'Worker Ownership and Section 8(a)(2) of the National Labor Relations Act', *Yale Law Journal* 91 (1982): 615–33.

variables, the main dependent variables being productivity, job satisfaction and earnings.

To consider the ownership problem more closely, we may distinguish among several different structures. The firm can be based (a) wholly on leased capital goods, (b) on outside nonvoting shares, (c) on voting shares with the principle 'One shareholder, one vote', (d) on voting shares with the principle 'One share, one vote', (e) on collective ownership of the firm's assets by the workers, or (f) some combination of the above. Of these (a), (b) and (e) are uncontroversially and unambiguously worker-controlled. To assess (c) and (d), we first define the ideal cooperative as one in which *all* workers and *only* workers hold *equal* shares in the firm. The ideal can be subverted in three ways. First, workers may own unequal shares. (In type (b) firms this is not a source of unequal influence on decision making, but it can be a source of unequal incomes if workers receive interest on their capital holdings.) Second, some shares may be held by outsiders who do not work in the firm. Third, the firm may employ some workers who are hired for a wage and who do not hold shares in the firms. The more one or several of these obtain, the more the firm differs from the ideal cooperative type and approaches the capitalist firm.

To have a quantitative expression of these distinctions, we may construct a Lorenz curve for cooperatives, as shown in Figure 1.1. In these graphs the percentage of workers is shown along the horizontal axes and the percentage of shares in the firm along the vertical axes. A point (x,y) in the coordinate system indicates that the x percent of the workers with the smallest number of shares have a total of y percent of the shares. The heavy lines represent the Lorenz Curves for different types of cooperatives. Figure 1.1A represents the ideal system in which all and only workers hold shares and the distribution of shares among them is absolutely equal. Figure 1.1B represents a 'subversion of the first kind'. Here all and only workers hold shares, but some hold more shares than others. Figure 1.1C represents a 'subversion of the second kind', in which all workers hold shares, but there are some nonworking shareholders. Figure 1.1D represents a 'subversion of the third kind', in which only workers hold shares but there are some nonshareholding workers. Figure 1.1E represents a combination of the second and third types. In Figure 1.1F all three subversions occur.

A possible index (the 'Gini index') of the degree of worker ownership is the ratio of the shaded area to the area under the 45° line. Using this index, Figures 1.1B, C and D are seen to be approximately equal in the

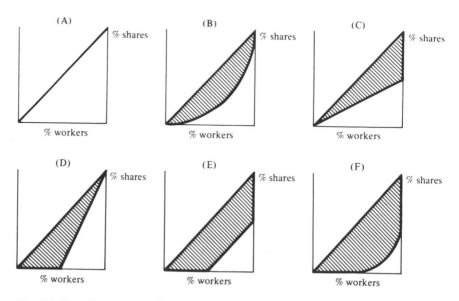

Fig. 1.1 This diagrammatic device is taken from N. Mygind, 'Are Self-Managed Firms Efficient? The Experience of the Danish Fully and Partly Self-Managed Firms' (mimeo), Copenhagen School of Business, January 1985.

extent to which they approach the ideal type. They all deviate from it to an equal extent, but for different reasons. If another index were used, they might differ in their approximation to the ideal.[57] Obviously, there is no 'correct' index in an absolute sense. The choice of index depends on the variable one wants to explain. If one's hypothesis is that the productivity-increasing effects of worker ownership depend mainly on all workers having a share, the Gini index, which makes Figures 1.1C and 1.1D equal, is inappropriate.

What we referred to as subversions of the first kind are quite common under the American ESOP system. Here shares are usually distributed to employees proportionally to their salaries, and the voting power is proportional to the number of shares. In practice, this amounts to the management's retaining a dominant influence in all important decisions. There is evidence that internal relations in such firms are more conflictual than they are in ordinary capitalist enterprises.[58] Subversions of the second kind are cited by Derek Jones in his study of British cooperatives. The outside shareholders in this case are largely former workers, other

[57]For an extensive discussion of different measures of inequality see A. Sen, *On Economic Inequality* (New York: Oxford University Press, 1973).
[58]See Note, 'Worker Ownership'.

cooperatives and trade unions.[59] Probably the most important, however, are subversions of the third kind. In the history of cooperatives one finds many examples of failure by success: A prosperous cooperative is easily tempted to employ wage labour instead of inviting other cooperators to share the earnings.[60] The best-known American cooperatives, plywood firms, employ hired workers quite extensively.[61] Although some of these are (well-paid) specialists who are hired for specific jobs, many apparently perform the same jobs as the coop members. Consistent with this practice, the attitude of the members is reported to be highly individualistic and nonideological.

Ownership structures of type (a), (b) or (e), and structures of type (c) or (d) with a low Gini index, make it possible for workers to control economic decisions, but cannot ensure the reality of democratic control. Labour cooperatives vary widely in the extent to which workers actually shape firm policies. If cooperatives are run on traditional hierarchical lines, the cause may be a failure of the democratic process. Large cooperatives, in particular, are vulnerable to the 'iron law of oligarchy'. In addition to the problems inherent in any large organization, cooperatives are constrained by efficiency considerations, which can make extensive participation impractical. It may also be, however, that the cooperative members have decided democratically that the day-to-day or even month-to-month operations of the enterprise should not be run on democratic lines. As long as the members do not abdicate their fundamental right to govern the enterprise, they can choose to have very widespread delegation of powers.

Cooperatives have wide scope for experimenting with different forms, guided by the principle that the best easily becomes the enemy of the good. Extensive application of direct democracy could lead either to bankruptcy or to the emergence of an informal elite. Representative democracy, with periodically elected managers who between elections have essentially the same powers as managers of capitalist firms, might be the best solution in many cases. If managers want to be reappointed, they will have to respect the interests of the rank and file. Because of 'the law of anticipated reactions', it may not be possible to detect 'truly' worker-controlled enterprises simply by looking at the formal distribu-

---

[59]Jones, 'British Producer Cooperatives'. Other examples are cited in Miller, 'Market Neutrality', p. 311.
[60]Miller, 'Market Neutrality'.
[61]According to Gunn, 'Workers' Self-Management', p. 101, hired workers in the eleven cooperatives in operation in 1982 represented about 25% of the total work force.

tion of short-term decision-making power. The long-term decision-making powers associated with ownership are probably more relevant.

1.3.2 What is market socialism?

Our use of the term 'market socialism' differs from that of some other writers. Oscar Lange, for example, considers market socialism to be a system of hierarchically organised firms owned by the state with managers hired on a profit-bonus arrangement.[62] The managers maximise profits with respect to prices set by the planning authorities. Lange argues that this system will more easily reach a general equilibrium with efficient resource utilisation than a fully decentralised market economy, which has no planning authorities that can act in the role of the market auctioneer.

Our concept of market socialism, by contrast, is that of a system of labour cooperatives. The system, however, need not cover all economic activities. Although one could imagine a market economy in which all firms were cooperatives and all economic activities took place in the market, nobody would advocate a system of this kind. Some productive and regulatory activities would have to be carried out by the state, as they are in all contemporary capitalist economies. More controversially, there could be room for traditional capitalist enterprises alongside the cooperative ones. Market socialism could even be compatible with the cooperatives being in a minority, if they interacted to form a substantial cooperative bloc in the economy. There is an enormous difference between the group of Mondragon cooperatives, about seventy altogether including a cooperative bank, and an isolated labour-managed firm in a wholly capitalist environment.

Several arguments could be advanced for a mixed system of capitalist and self-managed firms. First, there is the argument from economic freedom, discussed earlier. If some workers prefer working in capitalist firms, why not let them be allowed to do so? In the absence of externalities, there are no good reasons to deny them this option. It may well be that the workers attracted by the cooperative form a small subset of a heterogeneous labour force. Moreover, even if workers are homogeneous, they might be attracted by the notion of belonging to a small (but not too small) subset of the working population. The feeling of belonging to an *elite community* might be crucial – the elite aspect implying that the motivation would fall when their number grew too large, and the community

---

[62]See O. Lange and F. M. Taylor, *On the Economic Theory of Socialism* (New York: McGraw-Hill, 1964).

aspect that it would fall if their number grew too small. In biological parlance, this could give rise to a frequency-dependent stable polymorphism of capitalist and cooperative firms.

Second, the argument has been made that in an otherwise cooperative economy there should be 'a threshold size of enterprise, measured by the number of employees, below which conventional capital entrepreneurship would continue to operate', since 'the creation of new enterprises to fill market gaps and to exploit new technologies is by its nature more easily undertaken (and therefore more likely to be undertaken) by an individual than by a spontaneous workers' cooperative sprung readymade from the dole queue'.[63] The argument seems bizarre in several respects. For one thing, it is against the traditional (and, we think, well-founded) view that the cooperative form is particularly well-suited to small firms. For another, it is easy to imagine the perverse and distorting incentive effects, including the tendency toward excessive capitalintensive production, that would be created by this proposal.

Third, cooperatives are not equally suited in all lines of production. Activities that are best carried out on very large scale may not lend themselves to a participatory form. Activities that place a high premium on entrepreneurship, because of rapidly changing markets or technologies, may not fit the collective framework for decision making. If the cooperative appoints a salaried manager, he will not have the personal incentive of the entrepreneur. It might not be possible to give the manager a share of the surplus that is sufficiently high to overcome this problem without also undermining the cooperative spirit. Finally, not all production processes lend themselves easily to the workers' monitoring of one another that may be a condition for a viable cooperative (see Section 1.3.3). Note, however, that in the long run these constraints need not be fixed. Labour cooperatives would have an incentive to channel technical change and factory design to overcome these difficulties.

1.3.3 Work incentives and productivity
There is a considerable theoretical and empirical literature that discusses the impact of cooperative organisation on work incentives and productivity. Whereas the theoretical discussions usually conclude that the impact is negative, many of the empirical studies find a positive effect. Both sets of argument are rather inconclusive. We shall sketch them very briefly, without attempting to conclude in favour of one or the other.

[63]Jay, 'Workers' Cooperative Economy', p. 26.

The main theoretical argument derives from a seminal article by Armen Alchian and Harold Demsetz.[64] Stated simply, in the absence of supervision, workers have no incentive not to shirk, and in the absence of property rights in the residual income (after factor payments), the supervisor has no incentive to supervise. The first part of this statement excludes the pure 'peer group' as a viable organisational form. The second part excludes what might seem like an easy way out: The workers could appoint one among themselves to act as the enforcer of their general will and to prevent individual free riding.

The problem is a standard Prisoner's Dilemma: It is better for all workers if all work hard than if none do, but each worker's preferred strategy is shirking. It is thus amenable to analysis in the standard framework for this question.[65] For reasons mentioned earlier, we do not want to assume that workers act out of solidarity, morality or other non-self-interested motivations. Among the self-interested motivations capable of leading to cooperation in a Prisoner's Dilemma, two stand out. First, in a repeated Prisoner's Dilemma fear of retaliation and hope of reciprocation give the individual an incentive to cooperate, provided that he expects to interact with the same individuals again in the future and that his rate of time discounting is not too high.[66] Second, cooperation can be maintained by the use of selective incentives, that is, by punishing noncooperators or by rewarding cooperators.[67] Both of these solutions presuppose that noncooperators can be detected. In the capitalist firm, the task of identifying and punishing noncooperators falls to the supervisor. If his reward is linked to his performance, he will also have an incentive to do so efficiently.[68] The link will be strongest if he is the sole residual

[64]Armen Alchian and Harold Demsetz, 'Production, Information Costs, and Economic Organization', *American Economic Review* 62 (1972): 777–95. See also Jensen and Meckling, 'Rights and Production Functions', and Williamson, *Economic Institutions*.

[65]For a brief survey see J. Elster, 'Rationality, Morality and Collective Action', *Ethics 96* (1985): 136–55.

[66]For more precise statements, see R. Axelrod, *The Evolution of Cooperation* (New York: Basic, 1984) and M. Taylor, *The Possibility of Cooperation* (Cambridge University Press, 1987).

[67]See P. Oliver, 'Rewards and Punishments as Selective Incentives for Collective Action', *American Journal of Sociology 85* (1980): 1356–75.

[68]Note, however, the following argument: 'A supervisor would appear to be poorly placed to detect effective labor, compared to the team members themselves, especially if cost considerations prevent him from watching his team more than a small fraction of the time. One reason is that his performance sample will probably be a non-random one, unless he can observe without himself being seen' (L. Putterman, 'On Some Recent Explanations Why Capital Hires Labor', *Economic Inquiry 22* [1984]: 171–87, at p. 174 n. 5).

claimant, but it may also be sufficiently strong if his career and promotion depend on the performance of the workers under his supervision.

If the workers can detect shirking and free riding among themselves, they may be able to achieve unsupervised cooperation by either of the two mechanisms mentioned above. There are a few snags, however. First, detection of shirking may not be costless. Depending on the nature of the production process, mutual monitoring may be more or less costly, in terms of production forgone or in terms of extra efforts. Second, imposing sanctions on co-workers may not be costless.[69] Informal social controls, ostracism and the like also impose costs on the controller. In fact, detecting and sanctioning shirkers can give rise to a second-order free-rider problem. It is better for all workers if all supervise one another than if none do, but the incremental reward to one worker as a result of his supervisory effort may be smaller than the cost.[70] Finally, if workers have a short time horizon or if the rate of turnover in the labour force is high, the conditions for cooperation in the iterated Prisoner's Dilemma may not be satisfied. Beyond the trite statement that it is an empirical question whether and how much these problems will prevent mutual monitoring by workers, we want to repeat a point made earlier, namely, that it may be possible to organise the production process to minimise these obstacles to cooperation.

The empirical literature suggests, but far from unambiguously, that cooperation and participation increase productivity. Cooperative firms usually have lower turnover of the labour force than capitalist firms.[71] Cooperatives often have lower rates of absenteeism,[72] and they have no production losses from strikes.[73] Other things being equal, all of these

---

[69] This refers to punishment over and above the retaliation implicit in noncooperative behaviour.

[70] Actually, the converse statement could be true, if each worker finds that it pays him to supervise his co-workers but all would have been better off without supervision because of the negative 'atmosphere externalities' it generates. J. S. Mill cites an example from a French cooperative, in which 'the tailors complained that [the wage system] caused incessant disputes and quarrels, through the interest which each had in making his neighbours work. Their mutual watchfulness degenerated into a real slavery; nobody had the free control of his time and actions' (*Principles of Political Economy* [Fairfield: Kelley, 1976], p. 790). We are grateful to Jens Andvig for referring us to this text.

[71] H. Thomas and D. Logan, *Mondragon: An Economic Analysis* (London: Allen & Unwin, 1982), p. 48; M. Conte, 'Participation and Performance in U. S. Labor-Managed Firms', in Jones and Svejnar (eds), *Participatory and Self-Managed Firms*, pp. 213–37, at pp. 224–8. The lower turnover rate in unionised capitalist firms compared with that in nonunionised firms also accounts in part for the higher productivity of the former (R. B. Freeman and J. L. Medoff, *What Do Unions Do?* [New York: Basic, 1984], p. 174).

[72] Thomas and Logan, *Mondragon*, pp. 49–52; Gunn, *Workers' Self-Management*, p. 143.

[73] In their thirty years of operation, the Mondragon cooperatives have known one strike. For details, see Thomas and Logan, *Mondragon*, pp. 35–6.

should increase productivity. Since other things may not be equal, we must turn to direct studies of productivity. Both the Mondragon cooperatives and the American plywood firms have an excellent record, superior to that of conventionally organised firms, over a long period.[74] One study found that productivity in the plywood firms is higher (a) the higher the effective participation,[75] (b) the higher the ratio of worker-owners to all owners and (c) the higher the ratio of worker-owners to the total work force, the first correlation being the highest and the third the lowest.[76]

In his study of British cooperatives in the footwear, printing and clothing industries, Derek Jones[77] used three measures of participation: the proportion of the board of management that is worker-members (P_1), the proportion of the labour force that is members (P_2) and the proportion of the members that is workers (P_3). In the firms he studied (especially in the larger ones) productivity was positively associated with P_1 and negatively with P_2. There were important interaction effects between participation and economic incentives (bonus paid to workers and return on individual worker ownership of capital). Whether P_1 or P_2 is used, bonuses enhance productivity both in low-participation and high-participation firms, whereas individual ownership is negatively correlated with productivity in the former and positively in the latter.[78] The last finding can be interpreted as follows: Since the incentives in question are collective rather than individual – that is, depend on the performance of the firm as a whole rather than on that of the worker who receives the benefit, it is not surprising that they require effective participation for their motivating power.

A special problem arises if we consider innovation in the wide Schumpeterian sense, which includes, but does not reduce to, technical change. As the residual claimant, the classical capitalist entrepreneur has a large incentive to innovate. The worker in the cooperative firm has a much lower motivation to innovate, since he captures only a small part

---

[74]Thomas and Logan, *Mondragon*, chap. 5; Conte, 'Participation and Performance'.

[75]This variable was an index comprising (a) the percentage of worker-owners who served on the board of directors during 1963–7, (b) the percentage of worker-owners serving on committees in 1963, (c) the number of board meetings normally held during a year, (d) the number of general meetings normally held during a year, and (e) the effectiveness of methods used to communicate minutes of board meetings to the worker-owners.

[76]C. J. Bellas, *Industrial Democracy and the Worker-Owned Firm: A Study of Twenty-One Plywood Companies in the Pacific Northwest* (New York: Prager, 1972). For reasons explained in Conte, 'Participation and Performance', these findings are somewhat ambiguous.

[77]Jones, 'British Producer Cooperatives'.

[78]In this study P_3 was used only for a marginal purpose.

of the gains. There are to our knowledge no empirical studies of this problem. The theoretical argument, however, appears to be fairly strong. It could well be that a low rate of innovation and, hence, of economic growth would be the Achilles' heel of a market socialist system. Louis Putterman has suggested, somewhat tentatively, that the difference between capitalist and cooperative firms might be smaller than the argument implies.[79] First, as the classical capitalist entrepreneur is replaced by the modern, managerial corporation, the gains from innovation are diluted. Second, for an ordinary worker a small gain might be more important than a large gain would be for a manager or entrepreneur who is already quite wealthy. Third, workers might, because of their intimate knowledge of the production process, perceive potential improvements that might be missed by engineers.

1.3.4 Financial structure

Existing labour-managed firms have a large variety of financial arrangements. Still more types exist on paper. Cooperatives can be financed internally or externally, or they may be organised in a way that requires no financing at all. The last solution is that of the pure rental cooperative, which leases its buildings and capital goods and pays the rent out of current earnings. Except for very labour intensive cooperatives, this solution is cripplingly inefficient. It creates strong disincentives against the use of firm-specific capital.[80] Also, the rent will be very high as the owners know that the firm has no incentive to maintain the capital properly.[81]

Internal financing can take several forms. Capital provided by members can give rise to tradeable or refundable claims on the firm, or it can become the property of the cooperative as a whole. In the latter case the incentive of members to invest in their firm depends strongly on how long they expect to stay in the firm and on the rate of return on investment in the firm compared with what they can get elsewhere. If a worker has money in a savings account and leaves interest to accumulate, he also retains the principal. If he invests in the firm, he will get an annual return on his investment but will not be able to get the principal back. Clearly, the rate of return on investment in the firm must be higher than the rate of interest on savings for the worker to be indifferent between the two. For a numerical example, assume that the rate of interest is 5

[79]Putterman, 'Some Behavioral Perspectives', pp. 154–6.
[80]Williamson, *Economic Institutions*, p. 33 and passim.
[81]Alchian and Demsetz, 'Production, Information Costs, and Economic Organization,' sec. 6; Jensen and Meckling, 'Rights and Production Functions', p. 480.

percent. If the worker expects to stay in the firm for five years, he will require 23 percent return on investment in the firm; if he expects to stay ten years, he will require 13 percent; if he expects to stay twenty years, 8 percent. Clearly, internal financing in such cases will tend to be suboptimal. This is often referred to as the 'horizon problem' of the labour-managed firm.[82] Under normal conditions, it could be very severe. (Note, however, that under conditions of inflation it might be less serious. If nominal saving rates lag behind the rate of inflation, investing in the firm might be preferable since output prices usually do keep pace with inflation.)[83]

The comparison above is with an idealised capitalist firm. If the workers are organised and have strong bargaining power, the investment and saving decisions of the capitalist firm are highly influenced by the wage policy of the local union. Here again the horizon problem might be heavily felt. Union members who plan to leave the firm in the near future will prefer to take out high wages in the present at the cost of low levels of saving and investment by the firm. As a consequence, long-run productivity will fall short of the optimal level. In addition, a policy of low wages to secure higher wages and more secure employment in the future can be a very risky undertaking for the workers, since they have no guarantee that the retained profits at the disposal of the employer will be reinvested in their firm.

Internal financing may also be arranged so that investment by workers gives rise to refundable or tradeable claims. Frequently, workers have to pay a fee upon entry in the firm, which is paid back upon leave or retirement. The entry fee may not accumulate interest. In some firms, like the American plywood industries, new members have to purchase a share in the firm at the current market price. Often, workers also have the option of investing part of their current earnings, which are then placed in individual and refundable capital accounts earning the market rate of interest. There could be a free-rider problem here: Each worker might want his fellow workers to invest in the firm, to ensure future earnings and future consumption, but for himself he might want to convert all his current earnings into current consumption. This difficulty could be overcome by having collective investment decisions, combined with individual capital accounts. A more serious problem is that workers might be ill-advised to put all their eggs in one basket. If they want to save, they

[82]For an analysis see E. G. Furubotn, 'The Long-Run Analysis of the Labor-Managed Firm: An Alternative Interpretation', *American Economic Review* 66 (1976): 104–23.
[83]Sacks, *Self-Management and Efficiency*, p. 82.

should rather invest in a diversified portfolio of holdings in other firms. 'The workers cannot gain from tying up part of their income in a risky asset that cannot be traded.[84]

External financing could take one of two forms. The firm could borrow at fixed interest rates or it could offer nonvoting equity shares. Heavy reliance on borrowing would be undesirable, especially in capital-intensive firms, since the workers would bear the full brunt of market fluctuations. James Meade has an instructive example:

> Let us call the TNLE [total net labour earnings] plus the amount paid in interest and rent to those who have supplied the capital the Net Value Added (NVA). . . . In a labour-intensive concern in which the TNLE was 90% and the fixed interest and rent only 10% of the NVA, a 9% fall in the NVA would cause a 10% reduction in the TNLE available for distribution to the workers. In a capital-intensive concern in which the TNLE were 10% and the fixed interest and rent 90% of the NVA, a 9% fall in the NVA would cause a 90% reduction in the available TNLE.[85]

The other possibility, nonvoting shares, might look unattractive to investors, since they would not be able to exercise voting power to influence the behaviour of the firm.[86] The cooperative would to some extent, however, be kept in line by the knowledge that it may need to attract more capital in the future. Unless present shareholders are paid satisfactory dividends, future sharebuyers will not be forthcoming.[87] Knowing this, present sharebuyers will not be deterred by the fact that the cooperative is formally free to reduce the dividend to zero.

1.3.5 Cooperatives and labour unions

Unions have tended to be sceptical about cooperatives, partly for good reasons and partly for bad. If cooperatives are subverted through unequal ownership of shares or through the presence of nonworking members and working nonmembers, the result may be the emergence of an aristocracy of labour traditionally opposed by unions. Part of the resistance stems from the understandable reluctance of trade union officials to embrace a system that would appear to deprive them of their raison d'être. This reluctance will obviously be even stronger if the main

[84]J. Drèze, 'Some Theory of Labor Management and Participation', *Econometrica* 44 (1975): 1125–39, at p. 1134.
[85]J. Meade, 'Labour Co-operatives, Participation and Value-Added Sharing', in Clayre (ed.), *The Political Economy of Co-operation and Participation*, pp. 89–108, at p. 93.
[86]Drèze,'Theory of Labor Management'; Jensen and Meckling, 'Rights and Production Functions', p. 487.
[87]Jay, 'Workers' Cooperative Economy', pp. 14–15.

point of the cooperative economy is to reduce the power of trade unions, as in Peter Jay's argument cited earlier.

Trade unions have sometimes played an important role in transforming capitalist enterprises into cooperative ones. When the Norwegian shipyard A/S Solheimsviken recently changed to a cooperative, the local union played a leading role in the transformation. In his book on cooperatives in the United States, Christopher Gunn discusses at some length the workers' takeover of Rath Packing Company, which employed several thousand workers and had annual sales of several hundred million dollars. When the firm edged close to bankruptcy in the late 1970s, the local branch of United Food and Commercial Workers International Union helped set up an employee stock wage payment plan, which gave the workers immediate majority representation on the board of directors and, after a few years, would give them a majority of the shares. After the takeover the union continued to serve as intermediary on issues of rights, seniority, work assignments, grievances and other routine matters. Relations between the local union and the parent organisation were strained, since the latter feared that the Rath workers' agreement to finance their stock purchase through wage cuts could serve as ammunition for other employers in the packing industry.[88]

If we assume that a labour cooperative has been established as a going concern, it is hard to see what the role could be for a labour union, especially if it is part of an industry-wide union that negotiates wages for the industry as a whole. Gunn argues, however, that the need for a union would not wither away:

In cases where full workers' control is established, the union can expand its role as representative of members of the firm. It can act as a counterforce to natural tendencies of almost any organization's management to concentrate on the health of the organization, sometimes at the expense of immediate needs and rights of the firm's members. The union can become an advocate for expanded democracy in the organization – for education of all members, including management, to the processes and responsibilities of organizational self-management.[89]

At first glance, the argument seems strange. Surely, 'full workers' control' must include the tasks that are here assigned to the union. In particular, the trade-off between the long-run 'health of the organization' and the short-run 'needs and rights of the members' is presumably at

---

[88]For more up-to-date information about this case, see T. H. Hammer and R. N. Stern, 'A Yo-Yo Model of Cooperation: Union Participation in Management at the Rath Packing Company'. *Industrial and Labor Relations* 39 (1986): 337–49.

[89]Gunn, *Workers' Self-Management*, p. 171.

the core of the self-management process. Why should one and the same group of workers organise themselves in two different bodies, engaged in conflictual bargaining with one another? One answer could be that, unless restricted by a union, a cooperative could be forced to engage in self-exploitation – for example, accept wage cuts, sacrifice good working conditions and extend working hours in order to survive the competitive process. If this argument is accepted, the need for a trade union arises not because of internal tendencies in the firm, but because of a collective-action problem generated by the competitive environment. Unions are needed to protect workers against mutually harmful competitive practices. Against this, one ought to keep in mind the possibility that unions would insist on inflationary wage policies and not simply content themselves with collective self-protection.

One may ask why unions are widespread in capitalist societies, whereas labour-managed firms are relatively few. A simple answer may be derived from the fact that, for historical reasons, unions came first. Once established, they recruited workers with entrepreneurial skills to leading positions. The union bureaucrats then acquired personal interests in preserving the existing ownership structure. Some support for this hypothesis can be found in the fact that, in countries with a very high degree of unionisation, such as the Scandinavian ones, there are very few labour-managed firms. Conversely, the most successful group of cooperatives, the Mondragon group in northern Spain, was established under Franco when there was a ban on unions. Following the same logic, we should also expect a rise in the number of cooperatives in countries, such as the United States, in which the degree of unionisation is currently decreasing.

Part I

Alternatives

2 Internal subcontracting in Hungarian enterprises

György Sziráczki

The ailing state of the economy in Hungary became obvious in the late 1970s when the country's external debt reached a critical peak. Since then, state economic policy has focussed on reducing foreign debt. Central economic management tried to achieve this objective by different means. For instance, it restricted imports, investment and domestic demand and kept the living standard down whilst economic control became more centralised so that the authorities had greater influence in directing enterprise activities. As a result, economic growth has fallen back to a low level and real wages have declined whilst the country has achieved a trade surplus, slightly reducing external debt. Despite stagnation, full employment has been maintained, demand for labour has fallen only slightly and enterprises have hoarded labour. The reason is that under the present system of central wage regulation the connection between a firm's performance indicators and the formation of its wage fund is very loose. Any deterioration in enterprise performance has only a very limited effect on wages and employment.

The policy adopted to reduce the country's foreign debt proved to be a symptomatic treatment. The enterprises in the state sector relied heavily on the state; their inefficient functioning and poor capacity for rapid adaptation to the market did not improve. Moreover, the restrictive character of the economic policy created more and more economic and social strains. To inject some flexibility into the economy and offset the effects

Funding for this research was provided by awards from Girton College; the ORS Awards Scheme; the Chancellor's Fund, University of Cambridge; the Faculty of Economics and Politics, University of Cambridge; the Cambridge Political Economy Society Charity; the MTA-Soros Foundation, Budapest; and the University of Economics, Budapest. An earlier draft of this chapter was discussed in a labour seminar at the University of Cambridge, where a number of helpful comments were made. I would like to thank William Brown, Werner Sengenberger and Frank Wilkinson for helpful criticism and suggestions.

of diminishing real wages on the standard of living, central management took various steps to stimulate market competition in the state sector and to establish a flexible, small-scale semiprivate and private sector. One measure taken by the authorities was the creation of new forms of small undertakings. New possibilities of partnership and cooperative management – based on associations of private individuals – were devised.[1]

In this chapter the organisational development most widely adopted in Hungarian industry is discussed. This involved the establishment of relatively independent work-groups inside state-owned firms on a subcontract basis.[2] The first section of the chapter outlines the development of the present subcontracting system. Section 2.2 contains a brief analysis of the reasons for the high productivity of subcontracting units and delineates some of the advantages the new system provides for workers and management. Section 2.3 compares the present Hungarian subcontracting arrangement with the inside subcontracting system used in industrial firms in the nineteenth century. This limited comparison focusses on the relationships between subcontractors and firms and among members within subcontracting units.

Sections 2.4 and 2.5 examine the new forms of bargaining that characterise the relations between the subcontracting units and enterprises and the trade unions' responses to the spread of subcontracting work, respectively.

2.1 The development and spread of subcontracting

New legislation, operative from January 1982, officially sanctioned the setting up of work groups, consisting of as many as thirty members, to operate semi-independently within the enterprise where the participants are employed. Literally translated as "enterprise business work partnership" (abbreviated in Hungarian as VGM), these groups utilise the parent enterprise's facilities and equipment to produce goods and services outside their normal working hours. The work partnership pays a corporate tax on its profit and a fee to the enterprise for the use of its

---

[1]For details, see Laki (1984), Galasi and Sziráczki (1985).
[2]The chapter is heavily based on field research I conducted in the steel industry in September 1985. The study included interviews with partnership members, low-level supervisors, personnel managers and union officials and an examination of enterprise documents and records. In addition, I visited authorities, union organisations and an employer association to collect the necessary information and statistical data. I have also relied heavily on earlier articles on the VGMs, particularly Gábor et al (1984), Laki (1984), Kövári and Sziráczki (1984, 1985a, 1985b), Stark (1985a, 1985b), as well as case studies by Szmicsek (1984), Román (1985) and Neumann (1986).

equipment. Partnership members share among themselves the net profit as personal income, which is again taxed. This means that individuals, at the same time and in the same enterprise, have two quite different employment relationships: during regular hours they are directly employed for wages and nonwage benefits whilst outside normal hours they work as members of VGMs for a share of their profits.

The central economic management had great expectations for the VGMs. They assumed that, first, work partnerships would be profit-oriented, flexible, small-scale work organisations and would therefore produce goods or services in short supply, primarily for the market. Second, VGMs would help to resolve production bottlenecks inside the parent enterprise and take over those activities and services that had a lower minimum efficient scale of production than the main activities or that generated irregular or infrequent demand for labour. Third, with the partnerships interested in making profits and organising their work autonomously, central economic management hoped that new methods of organising both production and labour processes would evolve that might be applicable during regular hours. Fourth, central political-economic management hoped that viable VGMs would provide reasonable supplementary income for some groups of workers within the state industry, thus offering them an acceptable alternative (and this would also tone down firm managers' opposition) to the liberalisation and widening income opportunities of the private sector.

The legislation and establishment of the first partnerships were given great publicity, raising further hopes. Some idealists regarded the VGMs as new elements of the future socialist work organisation, which would contribute to the development of a new type of cooperation between management and employees, and as a result, the wage labourer relation would be replaced by partnership relations, even during regular working time. In practice, however, not only were the idealists disappointed, but many of the authorities' moderate expectations remained unfulfilled. A key fact, to be discussed later, is that the VGMs are legally bound into a dependent relationship with the parent enterprise. Since cost consciousness among enterprises in the state sector has not improved and their demand for resources, including that for labour, has remained unchanged, it is futile to hope or believe that the VGM arrangement by itself can transform the work organisation of the enterprise. Rather, it is the VGM that becomes assimilated into the parent firm in some respects.

At first, many enterprise directors were unsure in their response to the new initiative. Enterprise managers were afraid of the fact that partner-

Table 2.1. *Growth of work partnerships*

Date	VGM units	VGM members
June 1982	566	5,700
December 1982	2,755	29,300
June 1983	6,281	64,600
December 1983	9,192	98,000
June 1984	14,136	132,900
December 1984	17,420	196,000
June 1985	18,988	213,400
December 1985	20,625	241,400

Source: Hungarian Central Statistical Office, special reports on small businesses.

ships, using enterprise equipment, would produce for the market and possibly become the enterprise's rivals, while the enterprise itself often faced production bottlenecks, labour shortages in some jobs and increasing uncertainty during the recession. Moreover, legal uncertainties about the position of the VGMs remained and, until these could be clarified, this caused some managers understandable concern.

As Table 2.1 indicates, however, since this initial period of assessment, the foundation of VGMs has grown rapidly and continuously. More and more enterprise directors have recognised that the provisions of law relating to work partnerships give them an opportunity to gain control over the VGMs as well as to evade certain aspects of the central wage regulation. The law sanctioning the setting up of VGMs stipulated that the prior approval of the director of the parent enterprise was a necessary requirement and that this approval could be withdrawn at the director's discretion. This makes the VGM dependent on the enterprise and enables the managers to use the work partnerships for the enterprise's own purposes. Furthermore, the contract price (often called entrepreneurial fee) paid to the VGMs for their products or services is not classified as a wage cost but as a different and much lower taxed cost. It is treated as an external transaction and appears in the 'other expenditure account'. Consequently, the enterprise can pay it without the strict restrictions that constrain wage costs, thus providing a means of evading central wage regulation. By doing so the enterprise is free to pay higher wages for VGM work than for work during regular or overtime hours. This gives the enterprise management the double advantage of being able to stimulate its work force through high wages and to mitigate some problems facing the socialist firm by exploiting the voluntary and self-regulated aspect of VGMs.

Table 2.2. *VGM units and members by industries, 31 December 1984*

Industry	VGM units		VGM members	
	No. of units	% of firms with VGMs	No. of members	% of total employees
Mining	470	80.0	5,955	5.3
Electric energy	459	95.4	4,715	12.0
Metallurgy	758	89.3	10,750	13.1
Engineering	5,007	74.1	53,748	11.5
Building materials	569	72.9	7,465	10.6
Chemical	1,036	58.6	12,805	11.8
Light	1,074	36.9	22,797	6.4
Miscellaneous	202	43.3	1,893	4.3
Food	978	66.8	13,717	6.7
Total	11,183	56.5	133,845	9.0

Source: Hungarian Central Statistical Office, special reports on small businesses.

Generally, the director or a high-ranking manager of a given enterprise indicates that he would like a partnership to form in a particular field of activity. Then the organisation of the VGM and the selection of the membership are left to the shop-floor managers, foremen and respected skill workers, who recruit the membership during free hours from a strong informal group in the regular hours (Stark, 1986). More and more firm managers have promoted the establishment of VGMs. As a result, both the number of VGM units and members trebled and doubled in 1983 and 1984, respectively. By 1985, roughly one of every ten employees in industry was a partnership member, whilst VGMs existed in nearly 60 percent of all industrial enterprises.

The spread of VGMs is uneven, however (Table 2.2). They are heavily concentrated in heavy industry, especially metallurgy and energy, where almost every enterprise has some VGM units and where as many as 12 to 13 percent of employees are involved. The VGMs are also mainly composed of skilled male workers; clerical and administrative workers are seldom members. In contrast, in light industry, which employs mainly female semiskilled labour, only every third enterprise has VGM units and the proportion of partnership members just exceeds 6 percent.

This unequal distribution of VGMs among different branches of industry can be explained by a variety of factors. The operation of VGMs has often had the effect of increasing costs for enterprises because pay levels are much higher for workers in VGMs than for labourers who work regular hours, whilst the productivity level of the VGMs does not rise relative to these pay differences.[3] This raises the crucial question of whether the firm is itself able to bear the increased cost caused by their VGMs, or whether it can shift this burden onto the buyers or state. In light of this, it is not accidental that VGMs are concentrated mainly in large companies, because it is these firms that can often influence the prices of their products and secure financial viability through state subsidies.

Other factors that contribute to the spread of VGMs are the firm's labour market position and the power of its workers. Large companies are usually located in industrial centres where the labour shortage is greatest, and their labour is predominantly male skilled workers, that is, the economically and politically strategic group of employees in core urban industry. As a consequence, the branches of industry dominated by large companies tend to use more VGM units than the small-firm sectors. In the state sector, 86 percent of firms – most of them large or medium-sized businesses – have VGM units, whereas in the cooperative sector, which consists of small firms, only 22 percent of firms have work partnerships.

Capital-intensive industry is better able to accommodate work partnerships than those sectors where total labour costs are high. A further influential factor might be the relative importance of the industry for the central economic management. For example, in the case of the steel industry, which is a loss-making sector with poor product market prospect and outdated technology, the production of export goods is vital for the reduction of the country's international debt. Therefore, the industry has received high levels of subsidies from central authorities, which, among others, has allowed it to expand its VGMs. These factors together seem to be sufficient to explain the unequal spread of VGMs in the economy.

While promoting the establishment of VGMs, managers explicitly cut off these partnerships from the market, keeping their work capacities exclusively for the firm, subject to the firm director's own prerogative. As a result, the vast majority of work partnerships produce goods and services exclusively for their parent enterprises.[4] Their activities are located in the main production processes of the enterprises, where the VGMs usually produce standard component items. Sometimes they

[3]The operation of a VGM, of course, does not always increase the costs for the parent enterprise, particularly when the VGM produces goods and services for the external market. These partnerships, however, are rare.

[4]Ninety-six percent of the total sales revenues of goods and services produced by the VGMs in the industry in the first half of 1984 came from sales to the parent enterprise ('VGMs in the Industry', 1984).

undertake special orders, which the firm markets. Other, though not so typical, fields in which VGMs are involved are maintenance, service works and plant building. But in whatever the field VGMs are involved, workers almost always perform the same, or very similar, jobs using the same skills as they do in normal working time.

The additional earnings that the members receive from their work partnerships are substantial. Hourly earnings in the work partnerships are usually two and a half to three times higher than earnings during regular hours (Román, 1983). In 1984, the VGM members' average monthly income, including wages and benefits from regular hours and payments from VGM work, exceeded 50 to 80 percent of those who had no access to VGM membership. Thus work partnership income has become an important, perhaps the determining, factor in income differentials within firms.

2.2 Work partnership as a new structure of incentives

Under full employment, workers during regular working hours have no incentive to avoid holding back their performance, since if they are caught and dismissed they can easily find a new job. In contrast, the higher-earning opportunity in VGMs coupled with limited access to membership induces workers not to shirk during partnership hours. In fact, all evidence suggests that productivity in work partnerships is higher (sometimes even 50 to 100 percent higher) than during regular hours (Román, 1985).

The incentive not to shirk, no doubt, has a crucial impact on job performance; however, other factors also contribute to this higher productivity. Some of the difference between enterprise and partnership productivity is due to the higher skill level in VGMs. Furthermore, inside contractors tend to have a great deal of 'social capital' (contacts and connections) in the informal network of firm organisation that can be utilised to improve partnership performance. The semiautonomous aspects of VGM arrangement also have a positive effect on work incentive and productivity. In VGMs the firm often controls the quality of goods produced and the meeting of delivery deadlines, but not the actual working time and work inputs performed by the members. Usually partnership members can then economise on working hours by working harder and better than before.[5]

---

[5]Sometimes partnership members can control to some extent their total working time

One of the most important factors contributing to the higher productivity of VGM workers is probably the better organisation of work. Members are free to organise the work themselves. In comparison with the hierarchically organised firm, the partnership as a self-managed unit usually lacks the rigid division of labour imposed by bureaucratic rules. This increases the flexibility of the use of labour. For example, it facilitates recovery from crisis situations (better adaptation to work stoppages due to machine breakdown, worker illness, etc.). The partnership form, in which workers can organise both production and labour processes and appropriate the fruits of their own labour more fully, is an important source of small-scale technical innovations.

The collective aspect of the system promotes a spirit of cooperation and solidarity. The incentives are group-oriented rather than individual; that is, they depend on the performance of the partnership as a whole rather than on that of the workers who receive the payment. Mutual monitoring, which can be easily carried out in a small work team, and the high penalty a worker would pay if he lost his membership prevent workers from taking a free ride on the partnership. As a legally separate economic entity, the VGM might give the impression that its members belong to an elite group of workers. This elitism perhaps implies that the motivation to work faster and better is strong.

Whereas inside contracting promotes higher labour productivity, the system fails with equipment utilisation. Workers are not interested in utilising equipment, or materials and energy, with appropriate care, since they are provided by the firm, free of charge or at a low cost. Consequently, partnership members are inclined to exhaust equipment and neglect repairs, leaving them to the firm at the contract renewal interval.

The spread of partnership work and its higher productivity do not entail a drop in performance during regular working time, since managers usually stipulate that the performance level of the VGM members, compared with that of the pre-VGM period, not decline. However, workers have no incentive to surpass this customary performance level.

(regular plus partnership hours). When workers in VGMs do the same work as they normally do in regular hours and the production process is fragmented (production of components, maintenance work, etc.), the work done during regular hours and that done in the VGM are practically inseparable. This makes it possible for workers to improve methods of work organisation and to increase their performance also during regular working hours. In this way the performance levels set by management for regular hours are met in a shorter time than a normal working day, and it is therefore possible for workers to begin their VGM work unofficially during regular working hours. By doing so partnership members can economise on their total working time.

Thus if management tightened work norms during regular hours to match partnership productivity, workers would hold back their efforts even in VGMs and nonmembers would probably leave the firm (Kövári and Sziráczki, 1984). The contradiction between the incentives of the firm and the incentives of the partnerships prevents higher productivity, including organisational and technical innovations, from extending to regular hours (Stark, 1986). Thus members of the work partnerships have a dual interest and a dual behaviour – wage labourers during regular working hours but semiautonomous entrepreneurs during VGM works.

For enterprise management, the partnership form provides a new means of resolving different types of problems. In a large number of cases, the main aim of establishing a VGM is to stimulate effort and to harness the work force. Membership in a VGM is restricted to current or retired employees of the firm. Therefore, a worker who leaves the firm would be forced to quit his partnership.

Thus VGMs are an effective means of reducing turnover.[6] The enterprise policy of replacing overtime work with partnership activity has the effect of economising on the wage fund, because the entrepreneurial fees paid to the VGMs are not drawn from the enterprise wage fund but are charged against the firm's other expenditures account. These savings, then, can be used to pay special bonuses or higher wages to labourers who work during regular hours. Alternatively, the overtime work formerly performed by VGM members can be 'granted' to those workers who are excluded from the work partnerships. This gives management an opportunity to tie young, ambitious skilled workers more closely to the enterprise and thus to win the loyalty of a broader group of workers in the firm (Kövári and Sziráczki, 1985b).

The enterprise manager frequently approves the use of partnerships at critical stages of the production process to eliminate bottlenecks, to gain control over the meeting of quality specifications and delivery deadlines and sometimes to reduce costs and improve the enterprise's adaptation to the product market. Prior to the VGM-age, special repairs, maintenance, production of component parts and other specialised activities were often "put out" to external contractors when management found itself in difficulties. (For example, some jobs were beyond the firm's

---

[6]For instance, at 'Goliath', a large integrated steelworks, the yearly turnover among some 1,100 partnership members in the central maintenance plant was only 3 percent as compared with 22 percent among nonmembers. In another integrated steelworks, 'Samson', the same figures were 2 percent and 18 percent, respectively, in 1984.

capacity or simply the firm wanted to save part of its wage fund for other purposes.) However, this could entail a high price because the small-firm sector was relatively underdeveloped, and the external contractors often had a monopoly on their particular product or service. With the establishment of VGMs, enterprises have made efforts to cancel some of their external subcontracts and prefer to subcontract to their VGMs since they are cheaper than the outside units.

Work partnerships also have advantages beyond immediate cost savings. First, VGM contractors are available on the spot, and managers can therefore save time in contract preparation. Second, VGMs consist of highly qualified workers who have a complete understanding of particular needs of the enterprise, as well as the skills required to do the work, which usually ensures that the work will be carried out reliably (Stark, 1985b). Third, managers achieve greater flexibility and production security because they can put more pressure on the VGM than they could on external contractors to meet quality specifications and observe delivery deadlines. Thus there is an initial shift from outside to inside contracting.

2.3 Subcontracting in comparative perspective[7]

Interestingly some VGM characteristics mirror the inside contracting system that was typical of the industrial development, when large-scale mass markets had already developed but the typical form of organisation was still small-scale production. I shall briefly describe this early capitalist subcontracting system, based on the examples of the British and Americal steel industry, and then compare it with the VGM used in Hungary today.

In the early capitalist steel plants, the production process was controlled by skilled workers, who combined manual skills with chemical and metallurgical knowledge to regulate both the flow and the quality of products. Under these circumstances, it was a general practice for employers to contract out the operation of the individual processes to

[7]This section of the paper originates from a series of long discussion with Frank Wilkinson on various subcontracting arrangements in capitalist economy and the VGMs in Hungary, and a subsequent paper (Sziráczki 1984). I was also influenced by a paper of David Stark (1985b) in which he made an excellent comparison between the VGM system and its early capitalist counterparts. My analysis of the nineteenth century subcontracting system is based on the work of Pollard (1965), Birch (1967), Stone (1974), Wilkinson (1977), Elbaum and Wilkinson (1979), and on a number of original documents which Frank Wilkinson generously put at my disposal.

skilled workers. As inside contractors, these skilled workers were responsible for organising production and labour processes.

The two basic elements of pay arrangements between employers and subcontractors were, first, a tonnage rate at which employers contracted out the operation of the individual processes to skilled workers and, second, a sliding scale, which automatically linked the tonnage rate to product prices. This amounted to a means of sharing business risks between employers and contractors. Any pay negotiations covered only the contractors, who then hired their labourers and paid them, from their own tonnage rate, close to the market price of labour. Thus the contractors' pay was based on output, and they benefitted from the productivity growth whereas they paid their crew at a fixed time rate. These pay arrangements and the contractors' managerial authority over unskilled and semiskilled workers gave the contractors a monetary incentive both to increase productivity and to drive underhands hard to extract the largest possible share for themselves from the total wages they received under the terms of contracting agreements – a process resulting in substantial wage inequalities between skilled worker-contractors and their crew.

Employers found contracting agreements advantageous, for several reasons. Because the firms were comparatively small when they started to grow, the subsequent stages of production were often poorly integrated, management methods were still elementary and employers faced difficulties in supervising men who occupied strategic positions in the production process (Polard, 1965). Contracting was advantageous for employers then because it allowed them to reduce costs by delegating organisational and supervisory responsibilities to skilled workers, whilst payment by output (the tonnage rate) and the use of a sliding scale rate simplified cost accounting (Elbaum, 1984).

Ignoring for a moment the fact that Hungarian work partnerships operate only part time as subcontracting units, we can see that they share some similarities with this early capitalist contracting system. Their contracts define the type, specification, quality and delivery date for any product. Payment is by result and takes the form of an 'entrepreneurial fee' whilst supervision is the responsibility of the VGM and is quite independent of the parent enterprise (Gábor et al., 1984; Stark, 1985b).

However, the VGMs have also some important features which markedly distinguish them from the nineteenth-century subcontracting system. In the early industrial system the movement in product prices was the main determinant of changes in the general wage level of contractors. In contrast, product market prices have little impact on the entrepreneurial fee paid by firms to VGMs because, generally, work partnerships do not produce externally marketable products. Labour prices, particularly in the local second economy,[8] however, do play an important part in the determination of the VGM pay level. The explanation of this is that, in the contemporary Hungarian economy, the state sector offers employment security but low wages, whereas the insecure employment in the second economy is coupled with relatively high incomes. For this reason, for the broad mass of workers the second economy becomes an important source of income supplementary to that from the state sector. This combination offers employment security and a reasonable income level at the same time. Therefore, if a firm in the state sector wishes to encourage its workers to invest this extra performance within the firm, the manager must pay them at the same level as they are paid in the second economy.

In the nineteenth century, British steel industry institutions developed in the form of joint boards of arbitration and conciliation, which regulated bargaining between the organised contractors and the employers and provided procedures for setting wages at the local level (Wilkinson, 1977). In the case of VGMs, bargaining over entrepreneurial fees takes place at individual plants in a fragmented fashion. Procedures for settling agreements differ from enterprise to enterprise according to the local situation. Nevertheless, in spite of this fragmented subcontracting arrangement, the management-partnership negotiating process is in reality a formalization of 'the behind the scenes bargaining that takes place during regular working time (Kövári and Sziráczki, 1984, 1985b; Stark, 1985a).

A further difference between the two forms of contracting system is that the nineteenth-century arrangement revolved around individual contracting, whereas the present Hungarian system is rather like a group contracting. The relations within the former unit were hierarchically organised; the bargaining and dispute procedures did not cover semi- and unskilled workers; the skilled worker-subcontractor had almost complete authority to hire, fire and direct his crew; the payment system that characterised this relation is aptly described in the terminology of the 'drive system'; the wage inequality between the contractor and the

[8]The second economy includes those small-scale plants, businesses and forms of income redistribution that lie outside the state-controlled system of production and income distribution.

workers beneath him was high; and this sharp demarcation was institutionalised and strengthened by the early unions, which represented only the contractors' interest.

The internal organisation of the VGMs is notable for the absence of the strict hierarchical structuring which typified nineteenth-century contracting and the present day socialist firm (Stark, 1985b). There is, of course, nothing surprising about this, for most VGMs are formed from well-placed, mostly skilled workers and have a fairly homogeneous membership. This does not mean that VGMs usually lack every kind of hierarchy. On the contrary, hierarchy inside the VGM unit is necessarily reproduced to some extent. It is usual for the VGM to elect one of their members as a representative. This person is given the authority to organise the work of the group and to represent its interests externally. This representative is chosen by a vote of its membership. In practice, this role very frequently falls to the partnership member, who, in his capacity as foreman or low-ranking manager, has the same responsibilities during the main working time.[9] This has proved equally advantageous to firms, low-level managers and VGM members. The firm has the opportunity to influence, through its low-level managers, the decisions and functioning of the VGMs. The low-ranking manager may have an important part in mediating between enterprise and VGM interests. In this way, the conflicts between the organisations can be reduced. The low-ranking manager also extends his supervisory authority to the partnership, and he has an active concern for his partnership interests, even when he organises and directs production during regular hours, which is also beneficial to the members of the VGM. Generally, to the extent that the VGM is integrated and assimilated into the firm organisation, the VGM increases its chances of securing a peaceful coexistence within the firm, although this may be achieved at the expense of decreased autonomy.

2.4 Bargaining between work partnerships and enterprises

Most VGMs fill the orders of their parent enterprises. In these cases, before a job is started a contract is concluded between the enterprise and

[9]For example, at 'Goliath', one of the largest integrated steelworks in Hungary, where more than 200 VGMs have been established, nearly 50 percent of the representatives in 'maintenance' and 'auxiliary' partnerships are low-level managers, while VGMs in the main production fields of the steelworks are exclusively headed by foremen and other shop-floor supervisors. For other examples, see Neumann (1986).

the partnership. The contract declares the work to be done, quality specifications and deadlines; the materials, machines, energy and so on that the firm will provide; and the entrepreneurial fee. The firm negotiates with each VGM separately. The bargaining level as well as the procedure for settling contract prices varies greatly from one enterprise to another. In each case, however, bargaining between enterprise and VGM focusses on the entrepreneurial fee. This is in effect wage bargaining, since both managers and workers calculate the entrepreneurial fee on the basis of earnings held to be reasonable. VGM bargaining thus occurs within the context of a set of earnings ratios: earnings within the VGM as compared with those of a regular job, with earnings in the private sector and so on.

Overtime pay is, in principle, the lowest limit for earnings below which the VGM will not contract. For management, the upper limit of bargaining is the price for which it can have the work done by external subcontractors, hired labour, or Polish workers.[10] In reality, however, bargaining, influenced by the economic and political atmosphere both inside and outside the firm, moves within much narrower limits. However wide this margin is and whatever procedure regulates the bargaining process, the fact remains that the new subcontracting system in Hungary provides an open bargaining channel over reward for effort in contrast to the hidden (informal) bargaining processes that take place during regular hours. Partnership members are thus involved in a new form of representation in which, moreover, the representative is directly dependent on and responsible to the members (Stark, 1985a).

Although the bargaining between enterprises and work partnerships is an open and formalized way of settling wages, informal processes, as they are widely discussed both in media and research reports, still play no small part in the relationships both between the VGM and the parent enterprise, and between partnership members and non-members. As an example, workers frequently use 'inside' information on the situation and needs of the enterprise to squeeze better rates for their partnership (Stark, 1985a). If the partnership's representative is a low-ranking man-

---

[10]The wages received by Hungarian or Polish workers hired by the enterprise are not higher than those of its own workers. Nevertheless, the cost of such labour, which is not met from the enterprise wage fund, is very high. In the case of hired labour the contractor firms exploit the labour shortage in the external market, and they can charge a substantial fee for the provision of their rented labour. The price of the Polish guest workers, who come to Hungary under an interstate agreement and are allocated to the enterprises by the authorities, is determined by the central authorities. In both comparisons the VGM is a preferred solution, because it is cheaper.

ager, they may improve their bargaining power even more because of his access to exclusive information. It is also necessary for the VGM to negotiate informally with workers outside its membership. The VGM's task cannot be completely separated from the operation of the enterprise and it therefore remains dependent on tool room, stores, maintenance, administration, internal and external transport and other services. These provisions are usually specified in the contract but effective mobilisation requires the cooperation of the employees providing the services. This may be unwillingly given because of the very high rewards of the VGM membership when compared with their own. In these circumstances it is usually necessary for the VGM to negotiate cash settlements for the services it requires on a 'pocket to pocket' basis from funds the members make available to their representative (Stark, 1985b). If the partnership's representative is a low-level manager, these transactions can be eliminated. The manager can instruct the nonmember to carry out the support activity, or more frequently the manager will secure a nonmember's cooperation by allocating him special bonuses for the job. Generally speaking, at the interface of the firm and VGM, bilateral informal bargaining processes develop to facilitate the various exchange relations between the two work organisations, since these organisations operate on the basis of different incentive principles. Informal bargaining and side payment are inevitable.

A crucial problem with internal subcontracting is that since bargaining relations between a firm and its VGMs, in a given field of activity, necessarily involve only a small number of individuals, monopoly problems might abound.[11] In response to these problems, during the early period of the growth of VGMs some firms attempted to create a situation in which VGMs competed and thereby reduced the contract price. Thus to promote the competition between VGMs, management encouraged and supported the formation of as many VGMs as possible. Such a policy was adopted, for exmple, for some jobs in one of Hungary's largest enterprises, studied by Stark (1986). This policy introduced by management in some firms looked well in theory, but practice showed otherwise. Initially, as hoped, cutthroat competition developed and contract price declined, but this backfired in several ways. First, bitter conflicts between the VGMs culminated (in some instances) in inter-VGM sabotage, in an attempt to show that competitors were incapable of produc-

[11]This is a common problem with any kind of internal contracting work; see Williamson (1985).

ing quality work. Second, price became so low that managers had little faith that the products would meet the specification.

Third, the uncertain prospects for successive contracts discouraged workers from introducing innovations in the production process and utilising equipment with appropriate care. Those equipment repairs, for example, for which the benefits could be recovered only if the partnerships won the bid for successive contracts were delayed and left to the firm, leading to equipment abuse and neglect. Fourth, some work teams threatened to leave the enterprise altogether, an outcome totally opposed to the initial purpose of the VGMs, which was to keep workers by securing high additional incomes through VGMs. For these reasons the management's response was to reduce the number of VGM units and to divide the market, assigning each partnership to its own territory and restoring the price to the precompetition level.[12]

In another firm that I studied, the manager's attempt to create a market within the enterprise also failed, but not because of fierce competition. In fact, in the maintenance shop in question, competition could not even develop because the partnerships formed a price combination. VGMs reduced their prices only to such an extent that they gave the appearance of competition, and then they decided among themselves, by means of a rotation system, which VGM would take the job. In the absence of continuous contracting, the problem of equipment abuse remained, however.

These two examples show that in practice market competition among VGMs inside enterprise may play a very limited role in the setting of prices for work partnerships. The uncertain prospect of continuous bargaining is a serious impediment to internal contracting. For this reason, management contemplates a long-term ongoing relationship with its VGMs. The danger is that the VGMs can engage in a series of bilateral monopolistic exchanges with firm management; not only does this absorb real resources, but prompt, efficient adaptations are delayed.

To avoid this side effect, the firm has a tendency to take control over its VGMs. For example, the management sets the partnerships' income and working time ceilings, it monitors the performance and income distribution inside the VGMs and it resorts to different methods to limit the scope of bargaining. One of the most popular methods is as follows.

In calculating VGM prices for any particular job, both firms and part-

---

[12]This example is taken from Stark (1986). For similar examples drawn from the case of a large integrated steel works, see Szmicsek (1984) and Neuman (1986).

nerships often look at the price guidelines (called *Kisipari árjegyzék*) for small-scale private industry. These guidelines are regulated by the central authority and published in a standardised form. They serve as a common scale by which many firms and VGMs try to navigate in the course of bargaining. The entrepreneurial fee for VGM work is then determined in the following way. The hourly pay agreed upon as a result of bargaining is multiplied by the time based on the work norm (at 100 percent), and this amount is augmented by the various taxes to be paid by the partnership. The contract prices calculated in this way are usually lower than the costs of external subcontractors, foreign workers and Hungarian hired workers but higher than overtime pay. The ratio of reward for the same work in the main job and in the partnership is about 1 to 3. The bargaining process outlined here is fairly typical, but just one of many that is used in various firms to set the fee for VGM work.

2.5 Unions and VGMs

In capitalist economies, firms may resort to outside subcontracting to free themselves from union-imposed restrictions on the organisation of the labour process. It might appear that VGMs in Hungary would provide a similar 'back-door' method, since workers, in their capacity as VGM members, are not considered wage-labourers. All aspects of their activity are governed by the Civil Code and not the Labour Code (employment law). This legal position has some far-reaching implications concerning the relationship between trade unions and VGMs. Trade unions do not have the legal power to intervene in the VGMs, nor into the negotiation between the VGMs and firms, nor even into the labour process within the partnerships. A rash interpretation of work partnerships as some kind of union-evasion effort could be misleading, however (Stark, 1985b). Unions do not usually impose severe constraints on managements in Hungary, and furthermore the legislators regarded the VGMs as entrepreneurial organisations.

   Trade union officials, however, do feel confused and threatened by these new measures, and the hottest disputes over VGMs have been those inside the trade union movement. To understand the unions' reactions to the establishment and growth of VGMs, it is important to be aware of the unions' structural position within the socialist system. Trade unions are strongly embedded in the hierarchically organised institutions of society, which gives them two basic but conflicting roles:

to aid and promote the achievement of economic targets, on one hand, and to represent the interests of employees, on the other hand. At the same time they have no means of promoting worker interests through industrial action and open political pressure. The simultaneous fulfilment of these two, often contradictory economic and social tasks, given such limited means, places unions in a state of constant uncertainty. In this situation unions adopt a policy of seeking to minimise conflicts between the two aspects of their dual role. Because of this, union officials oppose any measures taken by state authorities or firms, such as the formation of VGMs, that create social tensions and conflicts in work places and that might increase the uncertainty that unions face.

The unions' authority is seriously challenged by the VGMs. First, the increasing earnings differentials between partnership members and nonmembers strain relations within firms. Nonmembers are also afraid that the higher pace of work and productivity in VGM hours will lead to a tightening of the work norm during main working hours. In addition, the vast majority of employees have no opportunity to become members of VGMs because of the nature of their work. A further cause of tension is the abuse of the VGM system by members. Examples are the use of regular working hours to do partnership work and, where the VGM is directed by the same person who acts as the foreman or low-level manager during main working hours, the distribution of work by the manager or foreman to the advantage of the VGM.

Second, trade union officials at the industry level are afraid of relaxing their firm-level apparatus lest they lose control over their own organisations. For example, because of the growth of VGMs, the propensity for workers to take up low-ranking administrative positions in unions is decreasing because they have no time to fulfill these roles. Furthermore, the work partnership has opened up an alternative form of representation which has real bargaining muscles and proved at times to be more effective than the official unions (Stark, 1985b).

Third, workers' involvement in inside subcontract work is detrimental to many traditional union tasks, like organising brigades (Stakhanovite-type movements) to help meet production targets. The incentives to work for brigades are less attractive for employees than working for partnerships after regular hours.

VGMs have extended working hours, which also conflicts with traditional union values. Unions warned against self-exploitation and campaigned, without success, for a wage regulation that would make the recognised level of subsistence attainable within official working hours.

Because of the usually highly skilled nature of the VGM work force and the widespread self-interest of enterprise managers in the VGM, the unions were prevented from voicing direct opposition. Instead they have adopted a policy of trying to gain control over the VGMs; they have demanded a say in the granting of the establishment of VGMs. They have also tried, mostly with success, to limit the number of hours worked and the level of wages earned in partnerships in order to reduce tension between VGM members and nonmembers. In this controlled and modified form the VGMs are, for the time being, acceptable to the unions.

2.6 Final remarks

As subcontracting units, Hungarian VGMs are in some ways akin to the outside subcontracting system which is currently growing in numerous industries in the West. In these countries cyclical and seasonal fluctuation in demand, and market uncertainty arising from such causes as volatile trade, easy entry into the market and strong competition, can induce management to resort to outside subcontracting. This provides a means of reducing production costs and shifting part of the risks onto the subcontractors.[13] Subcontracting also increases flexibility by providing opportunities for prompt responses in the product market. In addition, VGMs are used in attempts to eliminate bottlenecks and reduce market uncertainties. Nevertheless, market uncertainties in Hungary have often reflected the lack of a flexible small-firm sector. For this reason, whereas capitalist firms use outside subcontracting as a means of acquiring flexibility, Hungarian firms attempt to accomplish this goal by establishing subcontracting units inside firms (Kövari and Sziraczki, 1985a; Stark, 1985b).

The VGM cannot be regarded as an organisation of entrepreneurial character. It is subordinated to the firm and isolated from the market. The work partnership does not require any capital investment, and its members do not bear any business risk. For enterprise management, inside contracting provides a means of harnessing and stimulating the work force through high wages. The management is thus able to resolve some urgent problems facing the socialist firm. For workers, the partnership system functions as a source of supplementary income in the state

13See, e.g., Rubery and Wilkinson (1981).

sector. The spread of work partnerships has had an important stabilising effect, in a political sense.

Whilst with economic stagnation the purchasing power of official wages and average living standards have declined, opportunities to earn supplementary income exist for a politically and economically strategic group of skilled workers at the core urban industry. At the same time, VGMs have made enterprise management as well as an important group of workers accept the government policy of a more liberal treatment of the second economy. This is because hourly incomes received in the VGM are nearly as high as those received in the second economy, but they are more secure. The price of this, however, is an increase in work intensity and an extension of total working time.

Whereas outside subcontracting in the West provides management with a means of evading restrictions imposed by worker organisations or state legislation,[14] inside contracting in the Hungarian firm is a means of evading central wage regulation and institutionalising a narrow channel into an open bargaining process. The relationship of subcontracting to direct employment in the West is similar to the relationship of the secondary sector to the primary sector in Hungary.

Most VGM members are skilled workers with high supplementary earnings from partnerships. From the perspective of segmentation, the increasing use of subcontracting has very different consequences in the West and in Hungary. In the capitalist economy there is an increasing demarcation between enterprise internal and external labour markets.[15] In Hungary, by contrast, the increasing demarcation exists inside the enterprise between primary and secondary labour.

Although work partnerships have a legal status as internally self-managed economic units, their autonomy becomes inevitably limited under the circumstances (dependence on the parent enterprise and contradictions between incentive principles). Low-ranking managers extend their authority to the partnerships whilst firms gain control over some internal matters of the VGM. Consequently, the partnership loses part of its autonomy and becomes assimilated into the firm organisation. Despite their limited autonomy the potential created by the form of work organisation discussed in this paper is undeniable. Established as a possible solution to the scarcity and managerial problems of socialist organisation, the VGMs have created a greater flexibility in work

[14]See, e.g., Dombois and Friedmann (1984) and Heseler (1984).
[15]See, e.g., Sengenberger (1981).

organisation and new forms of worker representation. To the extent that the new policy succeeded in its objectives, it cast further doubt on the effectiveness of a high degree of hierarchical control on economic activity.

References

Birch, A. (1967). *The Economic History of the British Iron and Steel Industry*, London, Cass.

Dombois, R., and Friedmann, P. (1984). 'Employment Policy, Labour Legislation and Labour Market'. Paper presented at the 6th Conference of International Working Party on Labour Market Segmentation, Budapest.

Elbaum, B. (1984). 'The Making and Shaping of Job and Pay Structures in the Iron and Steel Industry'. In P. Osterman (ed.), *Internal Labour Markets*, New York, Heath.

Elbaum, B., and Wilkinson, F. (1979). 'Industrial Relations and Uneven Development: A Comparative Study of the American and British Steel Industries'. *Cambridge Journal of Economics* 3 (September): 275–303.

Gábor, I. et al (1984): 'Második gazdaság és a munkások' (Second economy and workers). Research report, University of Economics, Budapest.

Galasi, P., and Sziráczki, Gy. (1985). 'State Regulation, Enterprise Behaviour and the Labour Market in Hungary, 1968–83'. *Cambridge Journal of Economics* 9 (September): 203–19.

Heseler, H. (1984). 'Die Ökonomie der Leiharbeit – ein neues Gewerbe macht Karriere'. *Mehrwert* 23: 7–35.

Kövári, Gy., and Sziráczki, Gy. (1984). 'Keresetnövelö (alku) stratégiak: a túlórától a VGMK-ig' (Earning-increasing bargaining-strategies: from overtime to VGMK). Research report, University of Economics, Budapest.

Kövári, Gy., and Sziráczki, Gy. (1985a). 'Túlmunka vállalkozásban' (Overtime work in undertaking). *Mozgó Világ* 11 (no. 1): 14–24.

Kövári, G., and Sziráczki, Gy. (1985b). 'Old and New Forms of Wage Bargaining on the Shop Floor'. In P. Galasi and Gy. Sziráczki (eds.), *Labour Market and Second Economy in Hungary*. Frankfurt, Campus.

Laki T. (1984). 'Small Enterprises in Hungary: Myths and Reality'. *Acta Oeconomica* 32 (nos. 1–2): 39–63.

Laki T. (1984). 'Mitoszok és valóság' (Mythos and reality). *Valóság* 27 (no. 1): 1–26.

Neumann, L. (1986). 'A munkaszervezeti megújulás lehetöségei a VGM-ekben' (Possibilities of work organisational renewal in VGMs). Unpublished research report, Budapest, Mümki.

Pollard, S. (1965). *The Genesis of Modern Management*, London, Eluard Arnold.

Román, Z. (1983). 'A nagyvállalatok és a VGM' (Large firms and the VGM). *Társadalmi Szemle* 37 (no. 5): 28–43.

(1985). 'A VGM-ek termelékenységi tapasztalatai' (Productivity in VGMs). *Ipargazdasági Szemle* 16 (no. 1): 31–48.

Rubery, J., and Wilkinson, F. (1981). 'Outwork and Segmented Labour Markets'.

60   *György Sziráczki*

In F. Wilkinson (ed.), *The Dynamics of Labour Market Segmentation*. London, Academic Press.
Sengenberger, W. (1981). 'Labour Market Segmentation and the Business Cycle'. In F. Wilkinson (ed.), *The Dynamics of Labour Market Segmentation*. London, Academic Press.
Stark, D. (1985a). 'The Micropolitics of the Firm and the Macropolitics of Reform: New Forms of Workplace Bargaining in Hungarian Enterprises'. In P. Evans et al (eds.), *State versus Markets in Word-System*, Saga, Beverly Hills.
Stark, D. (1985b). 'Markets Inside the Socialist Firm: Internal Subcontracting in Hungarian Enterprises'. Paper presented at the Annual Meetings of the American Sociological Association, Washington, D.C.
Stark, D. (1986). 'Rethinking Internal Labor Markets: New Insights from a Comparative Perspective', *American Sociological Review 51* (August): 492–504.
Stone, K. (1974). 'The Origins of Job Structures in the Steel Industry'. *Review of Radical Political Economics 6* (Summer): 61–97.
Sziráczki, Gy. (1984). 'Shop Floor Bargaining in Hungarian Firms'. Paper presented at the Conference on Work Organisation in Non-Capitalist Societies, London.
Szmicsek, S. (1984). 'Két év után a VGM-röl (On the VGM after two years). *Közgazdasági Szemle 31* (no. 10): 692–741.

3 Profit-sharing capitalism

Martin L. Weitzman

In evaluating comparative economic systems at a high level of abstraction, I ask four types of general questions:

1. Is the system reasonably efficient? Does it deliver a comparatively high level of output relative to its inputs? Does it motivate people to work towards increasing output? Does the system fully employ its resources, especially labour?
2. Is the system reasonably equitable? Does it provide for a reasonably 'fair' distribution of income?
3. Does the system encourage a high rate of growth of output? (Even a relatively small discrepancy among rates of growth will magnify over time into significant differences in the standard of living.)
4. Is the economic system supportive of economic, political and social diversity? Or does it tend to suppress such differences by forcing work activities into a single mould?

No existing economic system delivers outstanding performance on all of these criteria all of the time. In a famous passage, Keynes argued that capitalism, *provided* that it can deal adequately with involuntary unemployment and an inequitable distribution of income, is the best available system. His *General Theory of Employment, Interest and Money* was written, in a time of great need, to provide some solution to the unemployment problem. What was the essence of this extremely influential book?

When Keynes came to sum up the central message of the *General Theory* for the economics profession, in a remarkable but by now long-forgotten *Quarterly Journal of Economics* article of 1937, he began with a 'general, philosophical disquisition on the behavior of mankind' – under uncertainty. Here as elsewhere, Keynes made it abundantly clear that he shared Frank Knight's distinction. 'Uncertainty' did not mean 'risk' – that which is, at least in principle, reducible to well-defined actuarial probabilities. By 'uncertainty' Keynes intended, I believe, to convey the idea of 'ignorance' – that which is essentially due to insufficient or precarious knowledge of the mechanism by which the future is generated out of the past.

The Keynesian scenario looks out over an economic world that is rife with uncertainty. In that world, expectations play an important dual role as both a manifestation of uncertainty and a cause of it. Such expectations are arbitrary to some degree because they can be based on almost anything, including self-fulfilling expectations of the behavior and expectations of others. And, as Keynes pointed out, 'being based on so flimsy a foundation', these expectations of expectations are 'subject to sudden and violent changes.'

It follows that, although there may ultimately be some long-run forces drawing it towards full employment, capitalism may also have some deep-seated tendencies towards short-run instability. Unadulterated laissez faire is likely to be out of equilibrium much of the time, and even when it is in equilibrium there is no guarantee of its being in a 'good' equilibrium. Whether in a state of 'bad' equilibrium or merely in disequilibrium, such coordination failures generate undesirable macroeconomic consequences like unemployment, which can cause very significant welfare losses. By the ultimate logic of this Keynesian world view, then, the stage is set for some form of government intervention to recoordinate the economy into a better configuration. Any such government policy will inevitably introduce some microeconomic distortions, but as an empirical matter such losses will tend to be small relative to the enormous welfare gains from having an economy operate at its full employment level.

Such general considerations do not indicate the best *form* of government intervention to stabilize the macroeconomy. Indeed, we do not currently have a general, realistic framework within which a meta-issue like that might be properly addressed. Nevertheless, it is possible, I believe, to give some common-sense criteria for desirable forms of government intervention. It is my contention that economists have not been sufficiently imaginative in devising operational mechanisms or systems possessing advantageous macroeconomic properties. The usual fiscal and monetary policies are, to my mind, sledgehammer-like tactics for controlling unemployment and inflation. They do the job, but clumsily, by brute force – and they can leave a big mess afterwards. I think it is possible to find subtler alternatives that operate more cleanly and with a softer touch by taking a page from the book of Adam Smith.

A good mechanism for fighting unemployment and inflation should have several noteworthy characteristics. It should be decentralised, based on the natural microeconomic incentives of a market-like environment. It should work more or less automatically, keeping to a minimum the need for using discretionary government policy. And, in a highly uncertain world, it should be robust in retaining its desirable macroeconomic characteristics over a wide range of possible situations or circumstances – including some that are currently unforeseen.

Although many different market systems are in principle possible, I think it is useful to think of three broad prototypes. One is socialism – government ownership of the important means of production and central planning of the major economic decisions. Another is capitalism – private ownership of most means of production and market-oriented decentralised economic decision making. A third broad category, not much seen in practice, is worker-managed producer cooperatives. Each system has its own advantages and disadvantages and comes in many varieties. Each system answers somewhat differently the four classes of questions posed at the beginning of the chapter. I will not cover these large issues here. My own thinking is close to Keynes's judgement: Capitalism, provided that it can deal adequately with unemployment and income distribution, is, and this is an empirical judgement, a superior system. (The inability, or great difficulty, of a system of worker-managed producer cooperatives to absorb unemployed outside workers, as well as the problems I think such a system would have in maintaining an aggressive pace of technological progress because of incentive problems, makes it an unrealistic economy-wide option in my opinion, despite an attractive façade of industrial democracy.) In this chapter, I shall address a more narrow issue of examining the macroeconomic implications of alternative variants of capitalism.

I shall argue that a superior form of government policy for combatting unemployment and inflation in our economies is to encourage, through exhortation and special tax privileges, the widespread use of profit sharing. A profit sharing system has the potential to counteract contractionary or inflationary shocks automatically – while maintaining the advantages of decentralised decision making. And these desirable properties are robustly preserved throughout a variety of economic environments. At the very least, widespread profit sharing can be a valuable adjunct to traditional monetary and fiscal policies.

I believe we should seriously consider some new ideas about basic reform of the economic mechanism, because our old ways of doing things are no longer adequate. The premier economic malady of our time is stagflation. Despite some abatement of its virulence in the immediate present, we still seem unable to reconcile, over a reasonably sustained period, high employment with low inflation. Even when economic conditions are on the upswing, significant pockets of unemployed workers remain throughout the Western capitalist countries. Right now, for example, we are afraid to push unemployment down aggressively to more humane levels for fear of reigniting inflation. The policy-induced recession remains our only reliable method for lowering inflation rates. It is difficult to imagine a more costly, inefficient or unjust waste of economic resources and human potential. The hope is that profit sharing represents a way of building into the system the kind of natural resistance to unemployment and inflation that could perhaps disarm stagflation at its source.

There is a sense in which our macroeconomic problems can be traced back, ultimately, to the wage system of paying labour. We try to award every employed worker a predetermined piece of the income pie before it is out of the oven, before the size of the pie is even known. Our 'social contract' promises workers a fixed wage independent of the health of their company, while the company chooses the employment level. That stabilises the money income of whomever is hired, but only at the considerable cost of loading unemployment on low-seniority workers and inflation on everybody – a socially inferior risk-sharing arrangement that both diminishes and makes more variable the real income of the working class as a whole.

Why does a profit-sharing system possess superior macroeconomic properties that help to stabilise output automatically at the full employment level and make it easier to deal with inflation? There is not sufficient space in this condensed chapter to give a detailed answer, so the true seeker must be prepared to fight through longer and more technical pieces (Weitzman, 1983, 1984, 1985). But a shorter heuristic story, a kind of summary, can be briefly told here.

At some risk of oversimplification, let me give a concrete if highly idealised (and extreme) example of what I have in mind. Suppose that wages plus fringe benefits of the average General Motors automobile worker come to 24 dollars per hour. This means that the cost to GM of hiring one additional hour of labor is 24 dollars. The extra hour of labor is used to produce more automobiles, which are then sold to yield increased revenue. If the increased revenue exceeds the increased cost, more workers will be hired; in the opposite case, workers will be laid off.

Since GM is trying to maximise profits, it will take on (or lay off) workers to the point where the additional revenue created by the extra hour of labor is neither more nor less than the additional cost, in this case 24 dollars. The average revenue per hour of labor will naturally be higher, say 36 dollars, to cover overhead, capital, profits and the like.

Now imagine that the car workers agree to a different type of contract with GM. Instead of a fixed wage of 24 dollars per hour, they go for a fixed two-thirds share of GM's average revenue of 36 dollars. At first glance there seems to be no difference between the two systems, since in both cases the workers get 24 dollars per hour. However, GM's incentive to hire or fire is subtly but dramatically changed.

If GM now hires an extra worker, its revenue goes up by 24 dollars as before, but its total labor cost in fact increases by only two-thirds of 24 dollars, or 16 dollars. It clears a profit of 8 dollars on the extra worker and understandably wants to go on hiring and expanding output. Moreover, in order to sell the extra output, GM has to reduce the price of its cars.

The benefits for the whole economy are thus clear: The new labour contract means more output and jobs – and lower prices. Firms want to hire more workers for the same reason they would be keen to acquire more salesmen on commission – nothing to lose, and something to gain.

So what is the rub? Clearly the revenue per worker – and therefore the pay – has declined because the marginal revenue brought in by the extra worker is less than the average revenue. Senior workers who are not unduly at risk of being laid off might resist the plan.

However, this conclusion does not necessarily follow if a large number of important firms introduce profit (or revenue) sharing, because as each firm expands and hires more workers, total workers' purchasing power rises, and so does the demand for GM's products. Not for the first time, the sum of the economic parts adds up to more than the parts themselves. The conclusions reached from this example generalise to 'mixed' formulas of base money wages plus shares of per capita profit (or revenue). A profit-sharing system makes the marginal value of an extra worker exceed the marginal cost of hiring that worker, which results in a short-run situation in which the demand for workers by the firms will exceed the supply. Hence a profit-sharing system will tend to gravitate towards an equilibrium with excess demand for labour.

Somewhat more abstractly, consider a typical monopolistically competitive firm in a partial-equilibrium setting. Suppose the wage is treated as a quasi-fixed parameter in the short run. If the firm can hire as much labour as it wants, it will employ workers to the point where the marginal revenue product of labour equals the wage rate. This is familiar enough. Consider however, what happens with a profit-sharing contract that names a base wage and a certain fraction of profits per worker to be paid to each worker. Suppose these two pay parameters are treated as quasi-fixed in the short run. A little reflection reveals that, if the profit-sharing firm can hire as much labour as it wants, it will employ workers to the point where the marginal revenue product of labour equals the base wage, independent of the value of the profit-sharing parameter. (Note, however, that what the worker is actually paid depends very much on the value of the profit-sharing coefficient.) When a standard IS-LM type of macromodel is constructed around such a model of the firm, the following isomorphism emerges: A profit-sharing macro-economy will find itself with the same output, employment and price level as the corresponding wage economy, whose wage is set at the profit-sharing economy's base wage level. In other words, the aggregate macroeconomic characteristics of a profit-sharing economy, excepting the distribution of income, are determined (on the cost side) by its base wage alone. The profit-sharing parameter does not influence output, employment or prices, although it does influence the distribution of income. If the employed workers can be persuaded to take more of their income in the form of profit shares and less in the form of base wages, that can result in a Pareto improvement – with increased aggregate output and employment, lower prices and higher real pay.

When identical-twin wage and profit-sharing economies are placed in the same stationary environment, with competitive labour markets, both economies will gravitate towards the same long-run full-employment equilibrium. But then let us perform the following thought experiment: In the typical style of disequilibrium analysis, let us disturb each economy and observe the short-run reaction when pay parameters are quasi-fixed but everything else is allowed to vary. The profit-sharing economy will remain at full employment after a disturbance, whereas a contractionary shock will cause a wage economy to disemploy labour. It should not be hard to imagine why such characteristics make a profit-sharing system more resistant to stagflation.

The same point can be made yet another way. Consider the standard textbook IS-LM type of model. Aggregate demand is determined, via the appropriate multipliers, as a function of autonomous spending injections and real money balances. The price level is determined as a degree-of-monopoly-power markup over wages. Wages are treated as exogenously fixed in the short run. Given the standard IS-LM type of specification, the model grinds out (as a parametric function of the wage level) output, employment and the price level. It is clear what happens within such a model if there is a ceterus paribus money wage cut. Output and employment are higher, whereas prices are lower. Yet this is exactly what occurs when an economy shifts towards profit sharing. The base wage determines the fundamental macroeconomic characteristics of the system – when there is an increase in profit shares at the expense of base wages, macroeconomic performance improves without loss of real labour income.

I am aware that such short-run, fixed-pay-parameter, disequilibrium models will be unsatisfying to the economic theory purist, who will want a full-blown account of why one payment mechanism rather than another has been selected by society in the first place and who will not rest content without understanding on a more fundamental level why pay parameters should be sticky in the short run. Such concerns have a legitimate place. But I do not think they should be taken to such an extreme that we are inhibited from examining what would happen in disequilibrium under alternative payment systems before first having firmly in hand a general, all-encompassing theory of economic systems and disequilibrium-like behavior.

What about the possible objections to profit sharing? Several are frequently voiced. I believe they can be successfully rebutted, but I have space here to deal with only one, and that skimpily. The objection to profit sharing one hears most often from economists is that, compared with a wage system, it represents a socially inefficient method of risk sharing. (Isn't it obvious that under a wage system the firm bears the risk, whereas under a profit-sharing system the worker bears the risk?) In my opinion the reasoning traditionally put forward to support this 'insurance' argument is fallacious, being based on a partial-equilibrium view that does not take into account the radically different macroeconomic consequences of the two systems for overall employment and aggregate output. The fixed wage does not stabilise labour income. What is true for the individual tenured worker is not true for labor as a whole. A more complete analysis, one that considers the situation as seen not by a tenured, high-seniority worker who already has job security, but by a neutral observer with a reasonably specified social welfare function defined over the entire population, makes it clear that the welfare advantages of a profit-sharing system (which delivers permanent full employment) are enormously greater than those of wage system (which permits unemployment). The basic reason is not difficult to understand. A wage system allows huge first-order Okun-gap losses of output and welfare to open up when a significant slice of the national income pie evaporates. A profit-sharing system stabilises aggregate output at the full-employment level, creating the biggest possible national income pie, while permitting only small second-order Harburger-triangle losses to arise because some crumbs have been randomly redistributed from a worker in one firm to a whole in another. It seems difficult to cook up an empirical real-world scenario, with reasonable numbers and specifications, in which a profit-sharing system does not deliver significantly greater social welfare than a wage system.

The superior-looking profit-sharing variant of capitalism is practised, to some extent, in the immensely successful economies of Japan, Korea and Taiwan. Although these countries are not clones, their economies do share certain important characteristics. In each case workers receive a significant fraction of their pay in the form of a bonus. The bonuses are large, averaging over good years and bad about 25 percent of a worker's total pay in Japan and about 15 percent in Korea and Taiwan. The degree to which the bonus is actually determined as a function of current profits per worker varies from firm to firm and depends on the country. (For example, in some Japanese companies the bonus is almost a disguised wage, but this is not true for most Japanese companies, and it appears to be hardly true for Korean companies.) Bonuses, like dividends, respond to corporate earnings, but with a complicated lag structure not easy to quantify by any rigidly prescribed rule. Overall, there is very little question that profit-sharing is a significant feature of the industrial landscapes of these 'Japanese-style' economies.

Though it is difficult to quantify the exact magnitude of its contribution out of a host of reinforcing tendencies, the bonus system is almost surely one major reason (although, most likely, far from the only reason) for the outstanding economic performances of Japan, Korea and Taiwan. Their flexible payment system helps these economies to ride out the business cycle with relatively high, stable levels of employment and output. Their governments enjoy greater leeway for fighting inflation without causing unemployment. The variability of real pay per member of the potential labour force has actually been reduced. Over time, a more equitable distribution of income has emerged than is found in other capitalist countries.

I believe that we in the West, instead of giving lessons as we are accustomed to doing, now must be prepared to take a lesson from the East. We should consciously tilt our economies towards this superior variant of capitalism. We ought to adopt a new social contract that promises our working people full employment without inflation but asks, in return, that workers receive a significant fraction of their pay in the form of a profit-sharing bonus.

But, the typical economist will ask, why if a profit-sharing system represents a far better way of operating a market economy than a wage system do we not see more examples of share economies? After all, even in Japan, Korea and Taiwan only modest (although significant) steps have been taken in this direction. The rest of the advanced capitalist countries are predominantly wage economies. Why, if profit-sharing is so beneficial, does not self-interest automatically lead firms and workers in this direction?

The answer involves an externality or market failure of enormous magnitude. In choosing a particular contract form, the firm and its workers calculate only the effects on themselves. They take no account whatsoever of the possible effects on the rest of the economy. When a firm and its workers select a labor contract with a strong profit-sharing component, they are contributing to an atmosphere of full employment and brisk aggregate demand without inflation because the firm is then more willing to hire new 'outsider' workers and to expand output by riding down its demand curve, lowering its price. But these macroeconomic advantages to the outsiders do not properly accrue to those insiders who make the decision. Like clean air, the benefits are spread throughout the community. The wage firm and its workers do not have the proper incentives to cease polluting the macroeconomic environment by converting to a share contract. The essence of the public-good aspect of the problem is that, in choosing among contract forms, the firm and its workers do not take into account the employment effects on the labor market as a whole and the consequent spending implications for aggregate demand. The macroeconomic externality of a tight labour market is helped by a share contract and hurt by a wage contract, but the difference is uncompensated. In such situations there can be no presumption that the economy is optimally organised and society-wide reform may be needed to nudge firms and workers towards increased profit sharing.

This much-needed reform will not come about easily. Persuading workers and companies to change fundamentally the way labor is paid, in the name of the public interest, will demand political leadership of a very high order. Material incentives will probably be required, such as favourable tax treatment of the profit-sharing component of a worker's pay. Yet the benefits of full employment without inflation are so enormous, the increased income is so great, that we cannot afford not to move in this direction.

References

Weitzman, Martin L. (1983). 'Some Macroeconomic Implications of Alternative Compensation Systems'. *Economic Journal 93:* 763–83. (Technical discussion of the microeconomic foundations of profit sharing's macroeconomic properties.)

(1984). *The Share Economy*. Cambridge, Mass., Harvard University Press. (Intended to be understandable to the lay person.)

(1985). 'The Simple Macroeconomics of Profit Sharing'. *American Economic Review, 75:* 937–53. (Technical treatment of comparison between the macro behavior of wage and profit-sharing economies.)

4 The unclearing market

Tamás Bauer

The well-functioning market of textbooks brings about general satisfaction. Under market-clearing prices, goods and factors offered for sale are sold; the demand of each agent is satisfied by supply by others. Wage earners are paid wages that more or less correspond to their marginal contribution. Etc., etc.

Life is, of course, much different. Present economies are essentially mixed economies with elements of market regulation and nonmarket regulation, by which state regulation and the role of trade unions and other nonmarket organisations are meant. This general statement, however, does not justify *any* mixture. It is somewhat like cooking: Most dishes are mixtures of different ingredients, but still, some dishes are tastier mixtures than others.

Hungarians are fed by their politicians and economists, not the worst mixture, by far, either in the direct or in the indirect sense just used. Hungarian cooking is highly praised by foreigners visiting the country (to be more precise, by visitors from the West who can afford a good restaurant there), but the Hungarian economic system is also praised as a fairly good mixture by the British and by Poles as well. It is sometimes lauded even by Hungarians, not only by government officials but by critical economists like myself.

I am one of the many Hungarian economists who argue for less plan and more market in the economy. Following this goal and starting from a centrally planned economy, one must accept mixtures. In such mixtures, two principles (*dva nachala* in Russian) coexist: the principle of bureaucratic allocation governed by state priorities and that of market regulation governed by profitability criteria. So one has a mixed-price system with fixed and free prices: a mixed system of commodity transfers with centrally controlled allocation (*fondirovaniye*) of some goods and free trade with others; a mixed investment system with large projects and programs decided on centrally and decentralised investment decided on and financed by the enterprises themselves. In foreign trade, the mixture develops due to the existence of the two types of foreign trade: a barter trade at administrative prices and delivery quotas in the CMEA (Council of Mutual Economic Assistance or Comecon) turnover, where priorities defined more or less in physical terms prevail, and trade governed by essentially market criteria in trade with market economies. The experience of the three CMEA countries that introduced market-oriented reforms (Czechoslovakia, 1967; Hungary, 1968; and Poland 1982) shows quite clearly that some such mixture is unavoidable.

The coexistence of the two principles, however, is by no means peaceful. If market regulation coexists with administrative control, market forces will be in action, profitability criteria will affect the economic situation of organisations and people, but very often without clearing the market, without satisfying many people. In this case the market exists but remains, so to say, unclear and brings about dissatisfaction for many. This particular mixture will then generate peculiar conflicts, which, in turn, may undermine the readiness of many social groups to accept or at least tolerate reform policy. This is why the nature of the mixture requires analysis. In this chapter I confine myself to pointing out several important aspects of the Hungarian mixture that have generated conflicts in the past and are expected to generate further conflicts in the future.

4.1 The market structure

4.1.1 The state and cooperative sectors

The structure of the market in centrally planned economies is characterised by an extremely high degree of monopolisation. This is partly a consequence of the concentration of economic activities into large organisations and partly a result of the system of hierarchical 'addressed' planning, based on a correspondence between particular items in the central plan and the plan of a particular enterprise. The reform may remove the latter but cannot immediately eliminate the first. It may, however, allow free space for newcomers entering into any market segment, as it did in Hungary.

State and cooperative industry and trade have been highly concentrated in Hungary. No more than 715 state enterprises and 623 cooperatives were active in Hungarian industry, 120 and 156, respectively, in building industry and around 500 enterprises and cooperatives in retail trade in 1982. The average size of Hungarian enterprises has been as high as in the neighbouring small countries with central planning (Romania, and Czechoslovakia) and the size structure of the firms has been very similar too.[1]

The state and cooperative enterprises have very often been in a monopoly position. Industrial and some building enterprises have been the single suppliers of their products in the country, while most building and trade enterprises have had a local monopoly or oligopoly. A recent survey by Zoltán Román has shown that the share of the biggest producer from domestic production was higher than one-third in 509, higher than one-half in 419, higher than three-quarters in 323 and higher than 90 percent in 214 from the 637 product groups in 1982. The biggest three producers supplied more than 90 percent in 508 cases.[2]

The decentralising efforts of the government in the past few years have hardly changed this picture, because most of the establishments of the enterprises that have turned into autonomous enterprises manufacture different products. Consequently, competitive situations have not emerged as a result.

So far the Hungarian picture resembles that of the neighboring planned economies. It is different, however, insofar as formal profile boundaries have partly been removed. Several state and cooperative enterprises have entered new markets, sometimes competing there with others. Recently this has spread even to the so far strictly monopolised sector of foreign trade.

4.1.2 The private and semiprivate sectors
The existence of another pole in the market has been the most important peculiarity of Hungary. Private handicraft has never been fully liquidated in Hungary as in Czechoslovakia or in the Soviet Union. The number of private owners has been 36,000 in industry, 19,000 in the building industry in the late seventies and 9,000 in retail trade. The owners of private enterprises have employed less than one person on average.

In line with the official private sector, the 'auxiliary units' of agricultural and retail trade cooperatives, active in industry, building, retail trade and different services, have been at the other pole of the enterprise

---

[1]See, e.g., Eva Ehrlich, *Establishment and Enterprise Size in Manufacturing: An East–West International Comparison* (Vienna Institute for Comparative Economic Studies, June 1984).
[2]Zoltán Román, 'The Conditions of Market Competition in the Hungarian Industry', *Acta Oeconomica 34*, no. 1–2 (1985): 79–97.

structure since 1968. In 1978, more than 1,200 of the 1,369 agricultural cooperatives and almost all retail trade cooperatives had (sometimes several) auxiliary units engaged in industrial production, employing here more than 60,000 people. They have delivered a small but not negligible part of national industrial and building output.

Recently, this other pole of the Hungarian enterprise structure has been enlarged. Not only has the traditional private sector started to grow (the number of enterprises has increased to 44,000 in industry, 27,000 in the building industry and 22,000 in retail trade, the average number of employees has increased slightly above 1 and their respective share in output and turnover has also increased slightly), but new forms of small-scale business have also been introduced. Enabled by the new regulations valid since 1982, 2,400 new small industrial enterprises were founded in three years. (This figure includes 'small enterprises', 'small cooperatives', 'private economic partnerships' and 'civil law societies', but 'enterprise economic partnerships' and 'specialised groups' in industrial cooperatives that are active within the mother enterprise and hardly appear independently on the market are excluded.) Whereas state enterprises employed 1,800 and industrial cooperatives more than 300 people on average in 1983, the new small enterprises employed not more than 16 people on average. In the building industry, 2,070 new enterprises such as these have been founded, employing 13 people on average, as against 1,900 employees in the state enterprises and 280 in building cooperatives on average.

Let it be added that there were 285 small enterprises, 368 small cooperatives and 7,400 private economic partnerships in all nonagricultural sectors in the national economy (industry, construction, trade and services) as of late 1984.

The new small enterprises contribute a very small part of national output: 0.5 percent in industry and 1.5 percent in building. Their share is less than that of traditional private handicraft (1.5 and 10.6 percent, respectively) or of the auxiliary units of the collective farms. Less than 1 percent of all labour incomes have been earned in the new small enterprises. Nevertheless, they are extremely important as a new beginning, as representatives of another principle (*nachalo*).

Ten years ago I wrote a paper on the contradictory position of enterprises under the New Economic Mechanism, in which I distinguished between two classes of enterprises: large ones that are in a monopoly position, are made responsible for supply tasks and consequently have a relation to the centre similar to that under the old system, and small and medium-size ones with less dependence on the centre and a smaller possibility of influencing the centre because of the looser relation between their production activity and national plan targets.[3] If there exists such a difference between larger and smaller state enterprises, the difference is certainly stronger with respect to auxiliary units of cooperatives and to new small enterprises.

In the midseventies I interviewed a manager on a collective farm and asked him whether the farm's industrial unit made a profit. 'Of course, otherwise we would close it', he answered. This philosophy has been alien to state and large cooperative enterprises: Only a few of them have been closed because of insolvency. It is out of the question that anybody would be ready to subsidise the new small enterprises. They simply will not survive if they incur losses.

The other side of the coin is, of course, that if medium-sized state enterprises and cooperatives have more freedom in relation to national plans than the large ones and the auxiliary units of the cooperatives have much more than any state enterprise, the freedom of the new small enterprises is the greatest. Some of them (especially the private economic partnerships) are economic subjects, which really have only to observe law and pay taxes. They have nothing more to do with the authorities. They may be free from *nomenklatura*, they may not have a personal manager responsible to the political authorities, they may not have a party organisation at all. They must live and survive on their own: They have to find the customer and set an acceptable price.

What kind of activities are the small enterprises engaged in? They are active in all branches of the economy—in industry, building, trade, services. Obviously, they are not copying the activities of state enterprises and large cooperatives. Rather they are filling the holes left by those. They manufacture short-series high-value consumer goods and complementary products for the state industry. Their most important field is industries. Consequently, large-scale state and cooperative enterprises and the small enterprises very often have business relations.

One might think that in such cases it is the small enterprises that have to compete for the orders of the large ones. Sometimes this is so, especially recently, in the case of the new forms of small-scale business. In relation to auxiliary units of cooperatives and some small enterprises and private economic partnerships, however, the large state enterprise has

---

[3]'The Contradictory Position of the Enterprise under the New Hungarian Economic Mechanism', *Co-existence 13*, no. 1 (1976): 65–80.

often been the weaker of the two partners. As a result of the distorted size structure of enterprises, of the lack of small enterprises in the economy, those who are ready to supply components have still often been in a strong bargaining position. Whereas the large customer has not only needed their supplies but has also been bound by numerous rules and informal obligations, the small partners could always refuse without any consequence if the terms offered by the customer did not suit them.

But why does the large customer not choose another small supplier if the first one makes his offer under unfavourable conditions? Because another one can still hardly be found. Even the new organisations are often reluctant to fight for each customer and are satisfied with a small market share that could be easily increased. Or, at the other extreme, they may prefer to make a large amount of money in the short run, neglecting long-term business considerations, and therefore insist on high prices. This is so because they do not trust the government concerning the possibilities for private business and try to make as much money as possible and as soon as possible.

The experience of the auxiliary units in the seventies was not very encouraging: First they were stimulated, then discouraged by financial and administrative restrictions and later stimulated again. Both types of behaviour mentioned above (the first found in industrial units of collective farms, the second in the private sector) are justified by the attitude of the authorities, who allow the new forms to exist but do not guarantee their future and do not promote their expansion. This attitude is well illustrated by the following passage from the Guidelines of the Central Committee for the 13th Party Congress published in late 1984: Auxiliary activities attached to the socialist sector have developed.

Measures aiming to limit harmful phenomena alien to socialist economic activity, unfair business and profit making and to strengthen discipline were passed but their effects are hard to perceive yet. Why, then, should the new entrepreneurs follow a long-run business policy with reasonable prices and growing turnover? Why should they make efforts to grow and to gain more customers in competition with others if this growth may throw suspicion on them? If they grow, they soon may exceed the employment size limitation set for each particular form. In principle, of course, any enterprise may then be transformed into another one of another type (e.g., the single craftsman may form an economic partnership with someone else, the economic partnership may be transformed into a small cooperative and further into a cooperative and a joint venture with another cooperative or with a state enterprise is also possible), but these possibilities have not been experienced so far.

Consequently, even the private sector is not so profit and sales-oriented as it should be according to the textbooks. Business partners and the general public notice their incomes rather than their performance. Under the existing conditions, in most cases they are neither allowed nor forced to be aggressive in satisfying any demand. Despite their entry, the market of goods and services has remained without being cleared.[4]

4.2 Labour market and housing market

The reader may ask why the two notions of labour market and housing market are linked in this section, but it will be clear later.

4.2.1 Housing, cars and recreation

If one divides the average monthly wage of workers and employees in the socialist (state and cooperative) sectors in Hungary (5,000 forints in 1982) by the official exchange rates of the National Bank of Hungary, one arrives at such figures as £80, $100, DM 300, OS 2,000 and NOK 900. These amounts do not represent the real purchasing power of the 5,000 forints, but the wages and salaries in the state and cooperative sector are, in a certain sense, low indeed. The wage level was formed together with the price level thirty years ago, to cover expenses for food, clothing and some basic industrial goods and nothing more. At that time it was assumed that housing, transport and recreation would be financed by public funds and offered to the public at highly subsidised nominal prices.[5] The wage increases of the last thirty years have been sufficient to cover a considerable increase in consumption (real wages have risen by more than twofold since the early fifties), but wages still do not cover the expenses for the items mentioned above.

Neither do public funds. In 1983, only one-eighth of all new flats were built and rented to people at low rent by the state (local councils); the rest

---

[4]An excellent and original analysis of the interplay between the state and cooperative sectors and the second economy on the 'unclearing market', particularly their inflationary effect, is given by Péter Galasi and Gábor Kertesi, 'Second Economy, Competition, Inflation', *Acta Oeconomica 33* (1985): 269–93.

[5]This was recently pointed out again by Professor Mrs. Katalin Falus in 'A munka szerinti elosztás es a reform' (Distribution according to performance and the reform), *Közgazdasági Szemle 31*, no. 9 (1984): 1047–58.

was sold to people at cost-covering prices or built by them. In addition, opportunities to borrow money for financing the purchase or building of flats have also been limited. (I will return to this point later.) In the same year, roughly one-third of all passenger transport was performed by private cars bought by the owners at prices containing extra taxes and, again, without the possibility of borrowing. As for recreation, only half of domestic recreation took place in subsidised trade union and other hostels; the other half and tourism abroad is based on commercial principles, at prices quite high compared with earnings.[6]

The withdrawal of the state from these three fields has paved the way for the market. But the withdrawal has not been complete, and here again we face peculiar mixtures. With cars the problem is relatively simple: One has to queue for new cars, and consequently second-hand cars have relatively high prices in the free market. Privileged groups may buy cars without queuing at a 10 percent surcharge, which is still low in comparison with free-market prices. The efforts to limit free-market transactions with new and not very old cars have not brought any results.[7]

The market of domestic recreation has at least three different segments. Subsidised recreation facilities are offered by the 'socialist sector' at low prices, but there is a shortage of such facilities, and they are allocated administratively. Privileged groups have easy access to them, whereas the vast majority have only limited access. The 'socialist sector' also offers commercial hotel accommodations, but those who have limited access to trade union recreation facilities can hardly afford commercial accommodations, with the exception of camping. The demand not satisfied by the 'socialist sector' is covered by the supply of private rooms leased to Hungarians and foreign guests. Since tourists from the West are also part of this market segment, the prices are still too high for most Hungarians.

The most complex and important field is that of housing. The accessibility of flats differs and so do the financial conditions. Rented council flats are the most advantageous but the least accessible. The low proportion of these flats among the new flats cited above does not reflect their actual importance in housing. State-owned flats still constitute one-fourth of the stock of flats on the national scale but more than half of the stock in Budapest and 30 percent in provincial towns. Consequently,

---

[6]The Hungarian situation differs greatly from that of other East European countries. See my 'Note on Money and Consumer in Eastern Europe', *Soviet Studies 35*, no. 3 (1983): 376–84.
[7]On the Hungarian car market see Kapitány, Kornai and Szabó, 'Reproduction of Shortage on the Hungarian Car Market', *Soviet Studies 36*, no. 2. (1984): 236–56.

there exists a wide market of rented flats, the right to rent them from the local council being sold and purchased. The down payment is roughly half of the price of an analogous privately owned flat.

Access to privately owned flats has several channels. Flats built by the state for sale and mostly sold under favourable credit conditions are in short supply. In 1983, for example, only one of five applicants could buy such a flat allocated by local councils. These flats, consequently, have to be allocated administratively. Local councils and employers (enterprises, institutions) participate equally in this distribution. If one intends to build oneself, construction land on the free market has a much higher price than the sum paid for the use of state land, which is, of course, in very short supply again. If one loses patience and decides to rent a privately owned flat in the free market, the rent will be three to five times higher than the rent of council flats and certainly higher than the average wage.

The same flat may therefore have very different prices if bought and rents if rented. There is no indication that this mixed system helps the poor: Surveys have repeatedly demonstrated that groups with higher incomes have greater access to cheaper forms of housing than do low-income groups.[8]

A mixed system of housing, in which low-cost social housing was available to the young and the poor, and those who wanted better flats or houses in preferred parts of towns and suburbs and could afford them would buy or rent on the free market, would be accepted by the public. This, however, is not the Hungarian case. In Hungary, the vast majority, including the young and the poor, are forced to turn to the market. Acquiring a flat requires a downpayment, which cannot be saved from any income received from the state and cooperative sector.

4.2.2 Two prices of labour
István Gábor and Péter Galasi have, in their pioneering book on the second economy in Hungary,[9] connected the existence of the second economy (among others) with the housing system, in particular with down payments. If nothing else, the cost of housing forces most Hungarians to seek opportunities to earn money above their earnings from employment in the state and cooperative enterprises.

[8]An article demonstrating this effect of the mixed housing system is Zsuzsa Dániel, 'Public Housing, Personal Income and Central Redistribution in Hungary', *Acta Oeconomica 31*, no. 1–2 (1983): 87–103.
[9]István Gábor and Péter Galasi, *A második gazdaság* (The second economy) (Budapest, Közgazdasági és Jogi Könyvkiadó, 1981).

Here, however, the rules of wage formation are different. There are many sources of income classed in the second economy, and only some of them are more lucrative than earnings from the state and cooperative sectors. When I translate a book, my income per hour is not higher than it is at the Institute of Economics. (True, I am not a professional translator and I work slowly.) But one of my colleagues, a young lady who, in her 'free time', earns money by weaving carpets for a private boutique, receives about twice as much.

Rules are different, in two ways at least. Central wage regulation limiting wages in state and cooperative sectors does not apply to the second economy. On the other side, most people place more value on their 'free time' than on their eight hours of working time. There are, therefore, two price levels of labour in Hungary now: one in the first and another in some parts of the second economy. True, performance is often different too, but not by rule.

A few years ago the Hungarian government decided to legalise and integrate the second economy. Small enterprises, small cooperatives and private economic partnerships, as new forms of small-scale business outside the traditional state and cooperative sector, were mentioned in the preceding section of this chapter. Probably the most original innovation in Hungary, however, has been a 'form of small-scale business' *within* the state sector: enterprise economic partnerships. Some employees of an enterprise form an autonomous economic unit and as such work after the eight hours of regular working time for their own employer. Since they are an independent economic unit, they are not paid wages by the enterprise. Instead they sell their services to the enterprise, and the members share the revenue. Central wage regulation does not apply to them, and their income after taxation may be much higher than their wages. The conditions of the contracts are often adjusted to usual incomes in the second economy. (In some state enterprises the management has refused to allow enterprise economic partnerships to be formed, arguing that labour should not have two prices at the same time and place.)

The fact that the same people are employed in both parts of the labour market, and recently that the same employers also appear on the demand side, does not mean that communication between the two really exists. Though quite an important part of the manpower employed in the first labour market has entered the second labour market, another important part has not and hardly will be able to do so. There are, of course, strong informational links between the two parts of the market, but the two prices hardly affect each other. Still there is a labour shortage in the one and there may be a slightly prevailing supply in the other. (The latter is only a guess; it can hardly be checked.) We have a peculiar mixture again, that of an overregulated and a 'free' (probably underregulated) labour market with different rules and different prices. 'Clearing of the market' is certainly impossible. The satisfaction of some and dissatisfaction of many others are accumulating.

4.3 Some comments on a missing market

There are many reasons for the emergence of this mixture, of the doubling of the labour market, not to be listed here. Let me return to the one mentioned above: the other mixture, the housing market. One may add the two other mixtures, the car market and the recreation market, where consumers need amounts of money that they cannot save from incomes received from the state and cooperative sectors.

Let me return to the exchange rates and say that a two-bedroom flat in Budapest might cost something like £12,000–18,000 or $16,000–24,000 or DM 50,000–75,000 or OS 320,000–480,000 or NOK 130,000–200,000 in the mid 1980s. This does not seem so bad. And a Lada car, the Nova version, might cost £2,200 or DM 8,500 or OS 58,000 or NOK 23,000 – less than in Western Europe. The difference, however, is not only in the much lower Hungarian incomes, especially in the case of flats. The crucial problem is the limited availability of credit. The maximum loan granted by the National Savings Bank for housing covered roughly one-third of the price of the flat mentioned above. One could get an additional loan from one's employer, but this was a question of luck and additional bank credit at a much higher interest rate and, again, limited in amount. And then there were relatives and friends to borrow from . . .

Here I arrive at a market that is still missing in Hungary. In Western market economies, where the supply of money is decentralised, some percentage of the money to be lent is always available for financing housing, and people with safe earnings have no difficulty in raising credit for housing. (The interest rate is another question, of course.) The same is true in business: A reliable business firm has no difficulty in raising credit if necessary for a promising new undertaking.

The Hungarian case is different, however. The Hungarian mixture – in full accordance with the views of most protagonists of market socialism – does not contain a capital market. All savings are still concentrated in the National Savings Bank and used according to the preferences of the central plan. Since the economy is still a shortage economy, where the investment propensity of the productive sectors continues to be endless, and is not effectively controlled by anything or anybody, only a residual has been allocated to housing, and the population has been forced to oversave. Similarly, money has been allocated to enterprises in the form of distribution instead of commercial crediting. In recent years state enterprises and cooperatives have become entitled to lend to one another and engage in some profit sharing but, after all, a business enterprise is not a typical supplier of money in a market economy.

The crucial point, of course, is eliminating the shortage economy. But from the institutional angle, without creating a capital market and commercial banking that offers credit both for housing and for business (including the new forms of small-scale business), all the existing markets, like the housing market and commodity markets, will remain distorted and will not be cleared.

The first steps towards a capital market have been issued and even a bond market has been established. A transition to commercial banking has been initiated. Let us hope that it is not too late and that dissatisfaction with the unavoidable effects of the existing mixtures, of 'unclearing markets', will not prevent the next steps from being taken.

5 Strong unions or worker control?

Karl Ove Moene

According to social democratic ideology, worker control is synonymous with the existence of strong unions, whereas property relations do not really matter. The goals of labour are seen as being achieved via strong unions, and at less cost, since this arrangement does not require risky capital commitments by the worker. The logic of this stylised trade union point of view is critically examined in this chapter with a focus on the behavior of the firm.

Of course, knowing that the means of production are under private ownership does not completely identify the power structure within firms. Workers may have *strategic control* over certain variables or *strong bargaining power*, which can lead to substantial concessions by owners. There are limits to union strength, however, and worker influence exerted through pressure and threats may lead to perverse outcomes.

The content of the chapter is as follows: In Section 5.1, we define worker-controlled production activities and distinguish them from those with strong unions. We then focus on the short-run responses to price changes by the two types of institutions. One of the evils of wage capitalism, especially one dominated by strong unions, is the instability of employment. As Weitzman (1983, 1985) reminds us, even a small drop in the demand for output may lead to increased unemployment, causing further drops in demand, hence more unemployment, hence even further drops in demand, and so on. In Section 5.2, we discuss the short-run hiring and firing decision of a coop and compare this behaviour with that of a capitalist firm with fixed wages in the short run. In Section 5.3, we move on to more long-run aspects and analyse problems related to capital accumulation and choices of techniques. Under such circumstances the strategic behaviour of the union comes more into play. We then

Comments on a draft of this chapter by the participants in the Conference on Comparative Market Systems, Oslo, January 1985, and by Bruce Wolman are gratefully acknowledged.

ask: Does the interaction between union and management in a capitalist firm produce results that tend more to the coop result as the bargaining power of the union increases?

5.1 Worker control defined

A production cooperative with worker control is defined somewhat restrictively as follows:

1. Productive activities are jointly carried out by the members (who in this case are the workers).
2. Important managerial decisions reflect the desires of the members, who participate in some manner in decision making.
3. The net income (income after expenses) is divided among the members according to some formula.
4. The members have equal rights, and important decisions are made democratically by one person, one vote.

Points 1–3 are identical to a definition of production cooperatives offered by Pryor (1983). Point 4 is added to exclude some types of employment privileges contrary to the idea of democratic self-management, yet implicitly assumed in many models of labour management.

This definition of worker control does not formally require that capital be owned by the coop members. Outside owners such as stockholders, however, would likely have some influence on their firms' decision making, and point 2 of the definition precludes outside control. In the following, therefore, we shall have worker-owned firms in mind. The main difference between worker-controlled firms and firms with strong unions has to do with the existence of conflicting interests between labour and capital. The latter type of institution may fulfill some of points 1–4, but not all of them at the same time or to the full extent. Take point 2, for example: Workers can very well express their desires through participation in some of the decision making of the local union. A union, however, has a stronger influence on some aspects of the firm's decision making than on others. Typically, union influence is strong in wage settlements, but weaker when it comes to employment and investment decisions. Furthermore, point 3 is seldom fulfilled even though local unions may force a sharing of profits. It should be observed, moreover, that for our discussion it is important to distinguish between results

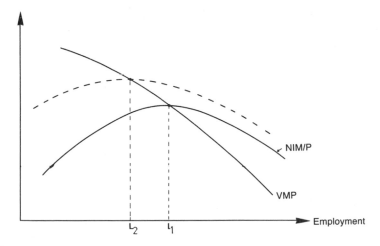

Fig. 5.1

obtained via accepted rules, on the one hand, and those achieved by force and threats, on the other.

5.2 Hiring and firing in the short run

There is an old argument that labour-managed firms in a market economy will have a perverse short-run supply curve: The higher the output price, the lower will be the supply. Ward (1957) was perhaps the first to point out that this anomaly followed from the assumption that the coop based short-run hiring and firing decisions on maximisation of the net income per member. This may be a reasonable goal to strive for in the long run, but as a description of what a coop will do in the short run it is (as many writers have pointed out) quite ridiculous.

Ward did not find reason to analyse a coop's day-to-day decisions any differently than its decisions relating to the distant future. Under this reasoning the coop will in the short run hire new members until the value of the marginal productivity (VMP) equals the net income per member (NIM). If VMP is lower than NIM, the marginal member contributes less that he is paid. Hence, NIM is increased by the firing of some of the members. The equilibrium point is illustrated in Figure 5.1, where the marginal productivity curve intersects the net income per member expressed in real terms (i.e., NIM divided by the output price).

What happens if the output price increases? In real terms, net income per member increases, because the fixed costs deflated by the output price decreases. Hence the NIM curve in Figure 5.1 shifts upwards, while the marginal productivity curve remains in place. As a consequence, the optimal number of members in the coop decreases and the firm's supply decreases the higher the output price.

This is indeed perverse short-run behaviour. Think of the situation in which the board of the coop announces, 'The output price has risen and our firm now earns more money than before; yet we suggest we fire twenty percent of our members in order to increase the income to the remaining eighty percent'. Who will vote in favour of such a proposal? Those who do must (a) be extremely selfish and (b) know that they will not be among the twenty percent who have to leave. Note, however, that the privileges inherent in (b) contradict the principle of equal rights or equal treatment of the members (see point 4 in the definition of worker control).

Equal treatment can be based on either ex ante or ex post considerations. In the latter case those who are forced to leave are compensated for their loss in income. In the former case there may be ex post inequality, but given that someone must be sacked, each member had the same probability of becoming one of the unlucky. One allowable procedure could be as follows: First, it is decided by majority vote how many members the coop should have; then those who have to leave are chosen by lottery. When the coop members vote, everyone knows the lottery procedure to be followed later on.

It can be shown (see Ireland and Law, 1982) that when the coop practices the principle of equal treatment in either an ex ante or an ex post way, no one will vote for reductions in membership when faced with higher output prices. This is so even when each member votes in a completely selfish manner and does not have an aversion to risk. Thus worker control does not imply a perverse output supply curve in the short run. It does not pay to sack workers after a price increase when those to be fired are going to obtain the same (expected) income as those who remain. However, the compensation or equal-treatment schemes introduced above do not, of course, reverse Ward's result: Faced with a higher output price, the coop will either reduce membership or keep it constant. The short-run response to higher output prices is therefore unchanged production.

According to Ward's theory, a *reduction* in the output price should lead to an increase in membership: fixed costs deflated by the output price increases, making it optimal to have more members share these commitments. However, since a democratically organised coop cannot fire members when and if the output price again rises, the coop will hesitate to take in more members. Accordingly, if the price drop is considered to be temporary, the coop has no incentive to respond by increasing membership. It may, however, be optimal for the coop to lay off some of its members temporarily when the price falls so much that the value of the 'last' producing member is below the unemployment compensation. The total income to be shared among the members will then be higher if at least one of them is placed on the dole while the rest continue producing in the coop.

In the appendix to this chapter, we are a little more precise about this short-run behaviour of the coop. Here the results are summarised and compared with those that follow from the case with capitalist control and unionised labour.

A typical feature of capitalist firms with unionised labour is wage rigidity in the short run. Maximum profit is obtained at an employment level where the VMP equals the wage level. A reduction in the output price leads to layoffs and to a drop in welfare for those who become unemployed. The capitalist firm has no incentive to take these costs into account. In contrast, a worker-controlled production cooperative internalises some of these 'unemployment costs' when it adheres to the principle of equal treatment of its members. As a consequence, the coop tends to have a more stable employment in unstable market environments than a capitalist firm with unionised labour. The capitalist firm tends to have fixed wages and variable employment, whereas the coop tends to have fixed employment and variable income. The capitalist firm distributes the consequences of recessions unequally between those who keep their jobs and those who are sacked. A coop is more likely to share the consequences of the bad times equally among its members.

Weitzman (1983) distinguishes between two 'tests' of employment stability: (a) Does a small drop in demand lead to increased unemployment? (b) Does an additional worker in the labour force obtain employment at once? A capitalist firm with rigid wages fails both tests, whereas a worker-controlled coop passes the first and fails the second. This means that, if a situation with full employment first has been reached, an economy with worker control will be less recession prone than a capitalistic wage economy. However, to avoid situations in which newcomers to the labour market are not absorbed, a sufficiently great reluctance to establish new firms is needed under labour management.

5.3 Long-run considerations: self-management versus bargaining

It follows from the preceding paragraph that the number of members to be chosen for a production coop should be considered an almost irreversible decision; ex post, membership can be increased, but not so easily reduced. Optimal membership should therefore be determined simultaneously with optimal investments so as to maximise the long-run net income per member. The optimality conditions are not so difficult to derive: The coop should

1. recruit members until the long-run value of the contribution of the last worker equals the long-run income per member, and
2. increase the amount of capital until the long-run value of capital's marginal contribution equals the unit investment cost.

When both conditions are fulfilled simultaneously, the coop is in long-run equilibrium.

The problem we now want to address is the following: Does the outcome of the decision making in a capitalist firm with unionized labour tend more towards the coop result as union strength increases?

An affirmative answer to this question may be found as a restrictive special case of the Nash-inspired bargaining theory of the firm (see Nash 1950). Models within this tradition are discussed by deMenil (1971), Aoki (1980), McDonald and Solow (1981), Svejnar (1982), Miyazaki (1984) and others. In this chapter we have in mind the so-called generalised Nash bargaining theory, where the outcome of the bargaining process is seen as a compromise between the two choices that the opposing sides would have made had they been all-powerful. Two characteristic features of the situation influence the compromise: (a) the disagreement or status quo points of the union and of the firm and (b) the bargaining power of the two.

The status quo points indicate the payoffs the two opposing sides can achieve if the bargaining breaks down. No one will agree to an outcome yielding less than his disagreement points.

Bargaining power is represented simply as a parameter $\gamma(0 \leq \gamma \leq 1)$ with the following interpretation: Assume that the union and the firm are going to share \$1 and that both are risk neutral. When the union obtains \$$\gamma$ and the firm \$$(1 - \gamma)$, the bargaining power of the union is γ and that of the firm $1 - \gamma$. The higher γ is, the more powerful the union.

Recent advances in bargaining theory have demonstrated a *possible* microfoundation for the generalised Nash bargaining solution. The solution of Nash's bargaining is shown to correspond to the equilibrium outcome of a strategic bargaining game in which the opposing sides are allowed to make credible offers and counteroffers (see Rubinstein 1982; Binmore, Rubinstein and Wolinsky, 1986). In this approach the bargaining power of one side is equal to that of the other, $\gamma = 1/2$, if the two sides are equally impatient to reach an agreement; that is, they have identical discount rates. If, however, the union has a lower discount rate than the firm, it becomes more powerful ($\gamma > 1/2$) and vice versa.

To describe the way the bargaining process is simulated both in a Nash setup and in the strategic approach mentioned above requires more technicalities than necessary for our purpose. Instead we shall list some conditions that are necessary for the outcome of the bargaining process to converge towards the coop equilibrium as γ goes to 1, that is, the conditions such that a capitalist production unit facing an all-powerful union behaves as a worker-controlled coop. Later, the realism of these conditions is questioned:

1. The union and the coop have the same maximand (i.e., the same preferences over employment, income, etc.).
2. The firm's disagreement point is zero.
3. All decisions about the relevant variables such as capital investment, employment and wage payments are made simultaneously and are binding for the lifetime of the chosen capital equipment.
4. The bargaining power of the union is 'exogenous'; the union cannot increase its strength via resource-consuming activities.

As already indicated it is not reasonable that these four conditions apply simultaneously. We shall now discuss them one by one and derive some economic consequences that follow when they are not fulfilled.

5.3.1 Union preferences
Many unions have positive preferences not only for high wages but also for the number of jobs. The reason may, for example, be one of the following: (a) The employed union members feel solidarity with the unemployed. (b) The union is guided by a principle of maximising the expected utility of a representative union member, where the probability of obtaining a job depends on the number of jobs available. (c) The union bureaucracy uses its discretionary power to improve its own status, which depends positively on both the income per union member and the number of employed members. Especially factors (b) and (c) and the fact

that the union often wishes to recruit new members, distinguishes union preferences from those that are likely to prevail in a worker coop.

An all-powerful union (with $\gamma = 1$) that wishes to obtain both high income per employed worker and a large number of jobs will choose a plant design other than an income maximising worker coop. Owing to the positive preferences for jobs, such a union wishes to have a production technique that is more labour intensive than a coop.

5.3.2 The threat points of capital owners

Whether the firm has a positive fallback profit depends, among other things, on the monopoly power of the union. The firm's fallback profit is zero only if (a) production cannot take place without the participation of the union members and (b) the capital owners cannot invest in other activities with a rate of profit higher than the rate of interest. When these conditions are not met, it is impossible for the union to squeeze pure profits to zero even though it may otherwise be all-powerful.

A positive fallback profit means that the property relations constrain the effective union strength. The capital owners can credibly withdraw if they do not at least obtain the highest payoff they can earn elsewhere. This threat has the same effect as a fixed cost burden leading a union with $\gamma = 1$ to choose a more labour-intensive plant design than it otherwise would have done. If the threat point can be expressed as a fixed rate of the capital that the owners provide, investments become more expensive. Hence a union with $\gamma = 1$ will underinvest as compared with what a coop would do.

5.3.3 Investment with short-term wage contracting

As a rule neither the union nor the firm will agree to binding wage contracts for the lifetime of the capital equipment. Such long-term contracts will not be obeyed anyway. It is difficult to obtain work peace within each short-term wage-contract period.

The natural sequence of decision making is therefore as follows: First, the firm makes the investment decision; next, the union and the firm periodically meet at the bargaining table to negotiate wages.

To analyse this kind of interaction let us proceed backwards. The assumption that the wage negotiations are settled according to Nash's (generalised) bargaining solution is maintained. The following question is then important: What will be the firm's threat point after the investment decision is made? Since the capital equipment can be sold for an alternative use, the union cannot press the firm's expected profits below the resale value of the equipment. If they did so, the firm would close down and sell the equipment. Accordingly, the *negotiable rent* will be the total sales income minus the resale value of the equipment.

This negotiable rent is an increasing function of the amount of capital invested as long as investments do not exceed the amount where its marginal product equals its resale price. As will be demonstrated below this will be fulfilled for investment decisions based on profit maximasation.

Now, according to Nash's bargaining solution, the union obtains share γ of the negotiable rent. As a consequence, the union's income with a given bargaining power will be higher (a) the lower the resale value of the equipment or, in other words, the more irreversible the investment decision; (b) the more fixed capital the firm has installed.

Let us then consider the situation the firm faces when it is going to make its investment decision. The firm then understands how the wage payment to be negotiated with the union later on will depend on the amount of capital invested. This dependence induces the firm to invest less than it otherwise would have done because each increment of capital will increase the wage payment to the union later on. Accordingly, the firm will invest less than the amount of capital that equalizes the value of the marginal contribution of the last increment with the unit investment cost. As was pointed out earlier, this is the investment criterion of the worker coop. The reason for the deviation is the fact that the wage increase accompanying higher investments constitutes an additional cost of capital in a capitalist firm where there are conflicting interests between labour and capital. Furthermore, the greater the union's bargaining power, the higher this additional cost of capital investment. Hence the underinvestment will be more serious the stronger the union.

A two-step bargaining procedure that is similar to the one discussed above has been analysed by Grout (1983). A paper by Crawford (1983) is also relevant, even though the problem addressed is more general. Crawford shows, among other things, that long-term relationships governed by short-term contracts do not yield Pareto-optimal outcomes. This also applies to our problem: If investments and income distribution were determined simultaneously, the payoff to both sides could be increased. However, the problem is credibility: The firm cannot trust that the union will refrain from using its bargaining power later on.

The firm also has an incentive ex ante to choose flexible capital equipment with a relatively high resale value. Namely, there may be a trade-off between productivity and flexibility in the plant design. The conflicting interests between the union and the firm can then induce the firm to choose less productive but more mobile and flexible equipment than it otherwise would have done.

5.3.4 Union strength and bargaining power

We have now come to the last condition that must be fulfilled for the collaborative solution to converge towards the coop equilibrium when union power increases. The question is whether it is reasonable to consider the bargaining power of the union as an exogenous parameter as is done in Nash's generalised bargaining solution. According to this theory, power and strength can be obtained without the expenditure of resources. In this way one is led to a rather optimistic view of a union's possibilities under capitalism. But how do organisations improve their bargaining position in real negotiations? At least three means are relevant:

1. By mobilizing their members and the public opinion to back the demands
2. By precommitment to certain irreversible actions, such as strikes and lockouts, so as to convince the opponent that his best choice is to yield (see Schelling, 1960)
3. By manipulating the relevant information

Considering such issues, Leif Johansen (1979) characterised bargaining as an inefficient decision system. He coined the phrase 'Bargaining has an inherent tendency to eliminate the potential gain which is the object of the bargaining' (p. 520). Worker influence via unions can suffer from this kind of social waste.

Let us consider strike threats as an example. A strike threat implies that the union is willing to act in a way that hurts both the workers and the capital owners. A precommitment to strikes may nevertheless be a rational strategy for the union, for the firm may yield to higher wage demands because of the profits forgone when a wage demand is turned down. The firm, however, would not be motivated to yield to every wage demand. By rejecting a wage demand and in fact letting a strike occur, the way may be paved for a profitable compromise for the firm, say with the payoff π_0 for the rest of the production period. The union must therefore not demand a wage level that, if accepted, would yield a lower profit than π_0. Hence if both sides were fully informed, the union would demand the highest wage level the firm would find profitable to accept.

So far this process is not necessarily inefficient, disregarding the mobilisation costs of the union. The strike threat is put forward, but the strike does not have to put into effect. However, at least two issues can disturb the picture:

1. The firm may have incentives to hide information about its true profitability in order to deter the union from demanding high wages. The union then has to put forward its wage demand without knowing exactly how harmful a strike will be to the employer. Such decision making under uncertainty implies a positive probability that the wage demand will be too high, making the firm's best choice *not* to yield. A strike will then occur (for further discussion see Moene, 1984, chap. 8).
2. The strike threat of the union will be more effective the more the firm has invested in capital. The profit forgone during a work stoppage will be higher the higher the productivity of the plant. Hence when the firm knows that the union might use a strike threat strategy in future wage disputes, it will again have incentives to underinvest so as to limit wage demands (see Moene, 1984, chap. 8).

Both 1 and 2 imply social waste and inefficiency. In addition, it may be profitable for the union to strike now in order to demonstrate its capacity for struggle and fighting. By so doing the union can establish a reputation as a tough bargainer, which may prove to be advantageous in later disputes. The effects of such a reputation may be taken care of by an increase in the parameter γ in the generalised Nash's bargaining solution discussed earlier. The point in this connection, however, is that activities that increase γ themselves influence the behaviour of the firm.

5.4 Concluding remarks

I have tried to make a case for the proposition that the normal behaviour of capitalist firms facing strong unions may be quite different from that of a worker-controlled coop. Under some circumstances the behaviour of the former type of institution will differ from that of a coop in direct proportion to the strength of the union. Underinvestment seems to be one of the main problems of capitalist firms with a unionised labour pool.

Regarding short-run behaviour, it was demonstrated that a worker coop has more stable employment than a capitalist firm with rigid wages. The tendency to underinvestment in capitalist firms strengthens this result: If the output price falls below the minimum variable unit cost, the plant will temporarily shut down. The less capital that is installed, the higher will be the variable unit costs and the higher the propensity of temporary shutdowns in a market with price fluctuations.

Appendix: the short-run behaviour of the coop

Let the initial number of members be N, determined in accordance with the long-run equilibrium, that is, where VMP equals NIM, as indicated in Figure 5.1. Furthermore, let Q indicate the coop's net income, which, of course, is higher the larger the number of producing members n; the increase in Q caused by a marginal increase in n being the VMP. A fired member receives a publicly financed unemployment compensation b. Finally, y indicates expected income per coop member (i.e., the NIM). The problem is: When does it pay for the coop to reduce employment, that is, to choose $n < N$?

In the case with ex post compensation, y is equal to net income minus compensation to fired members divided by the new number of members, that is,

$$y = [Q - (y - b)(N - n)]\frac{1}{n},\tag{1}$$

where $(y - b)$ is the compensation amount. Solving for y, we obtain

$$y = [Q + b(N - n)]\frac{1}{n}.\tag{2}$$

In the case with equal treatment, ex ante but not ex post y indicates expected income before the lottery,

$$y = \frac{Q}{n}\left(\frac{n}{N}\right) + b\frac{(N - n)}{N} = [Q + b(N - n)]\frac{1}{N},\tag{3}$$

where (n/N) is the probability of staying in the coop and $(N - n)/N$ is the probability of being fired. As we can see, (3) is identical to (2).

Now, a selfish coop member will vote for the value of $n \leq N$ that maximises the *net income per member*. From (2) and (3) we see that this behaviour in fact implies that total membership N is allocated between the coop and the dole so as to maximise *the sum of net income to all the N members*. Hence an individually rational voting behaviour leads to a collectively rational outcome due to the equal treatment or compensation

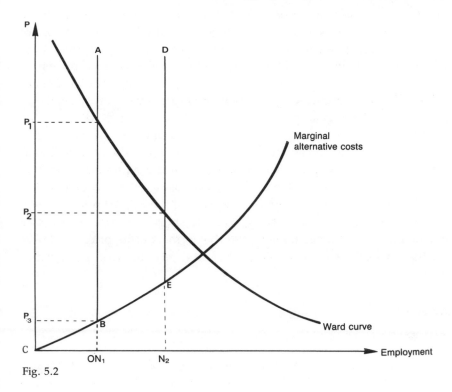

Fig. 5.2

schemes. Such a collectively rational goal does not lead to perverse results as will be demonstrated.

Price increase

Will anybody then vote for $n < N$? The answer is no: A price increase leads to a higher Q and therefore to a higher VMP. Furthermore, according to (2) and (3) it will be optimal to place some members on the dole only if the VMP with everyone producing is lower than the unemployment compensation b. Hence since initially $NIM \geq b$ (otherwise the coop was unprofitable) and since initially $VMP = NIM$ we know with certainty that the VMP with everyone producing must be even higher after the price increase.

Price decrease

Will anyone now vote for $n < N$? From (2) and (3) we see that y increases by reducing employment only if the output price has fallen so much that the VMP with everyone producing is below the unemployment benefit b. Hence since y in the long-run equilibrium is strictly higher than b, not every price decrease will lead to layoffs: There will be a price interval in which the employment of the coop tends to be stable vis-à-vis price fluctuations. The case is illustrated in Figure 5.2, in which the Ward curve shows what the optimal long-run membership is, given any normal output price. If the normal price is p_1, optimal membership is N_1 and the short-run response to price fluctuations is indicated by the curve ABC. When the price falls below p_3, it becomes optimal to the coop to lay off some members. The price is then lower than the marginal alternative costs of coop production, that is, the costs of using the last coop member in terms of forgone unemployment benefits. If the normal price were p_2, optimal membership would be N_2 and the short-run response to price fluctuations DEC. As seen, the higher the normal output price, the lower are the prices the coop can tolerate before it pays to layoff some members.

References

Aoki, M. (1980). 'A Model of the Firm as a Stockholder–Employee Cooperative Game', *American Economic Review 70*: 600–10.

Binmore, K., Rubinstein, A., and Wolinsky, A. (1986). 'The Nash Bargain Solution in Economic Modeling'. *Rand Journal of Economics 17*: 176–88.

Crawford, V. (1983). 'Dynamic Bargaining: Long Term Relationship Governed by Short-Term Contracts'. Discussion paper, University of California, San Diego, Department of Economics.

deMenil, G. (1971). *Bargaining: Monopoly Power versus Union Power*. Cambridge, Mass., Harvard University Press.

Grout, P. (1983). 'Investment and Wages in the Absence of Binding Contracts: A Nash Bargaining Approach'. *Econometrica, 52*: 449–60.

Ireland, N. and Law, P. (1982). *The Economics of Labour-Managed Enterprises*. London, Croom Helm.

Johansen, L. (1979). 'The Bargaining Society and the Inefficiency of Bargaining'. *Kyklos 32*: 497–522,

McDonald, J. and Solow, R. (1981). 'Wage Bargaining and Employment'. *American Economic Review 71*: 896–908.

Meade, J. (1972). 'The Theory of Labour-Managed Firms and of Profit-Sharing'. *Economic Journal 82*: 402–28.

Miyazaki, H. (1984). 'Internal Bargaining, Labor Contracts and a Marshallian Theory of the Firm'. *American Economic Review 74*: 381–93.

Moene, K. (1984). 'Investments and Fluctuations: Optimal "Putty Clay" Investments Under Uncertain Business Prospects'. Memorandum, University of Oslo, Department of Economics, 2 February.

Nash, J. (1950). 'The Bargaining Problem', *Econometrica 18*: 155–62.

Pryor, F. (1983). 'The Economics of Production Cooperatives: A Reader's Guide'. *Annals of Public and Co-operative Economy 54*: 133–72.

Rubinstein, A. (1982). 'Perfect Equilibrium in a Bargaining Model'. *Econometrica 50*: 97–109.

Svejnar, J. (1982). 'On the Theory of a Participatory Firm', *Journal of Economic Theory 17*: 313–30.

Schelling, T. (1969). *The Strategy of Conflict*. Cambridge, Mass.: Harvard University Press.

Ward, B. (1957). 'The Firm in Illyria: Market Syndicalism'. *American Economic Review 48*: 566–89.

Weitzman, M. (1983). 'Some Macroeconomic Implications of Alternative Compensation Systems'. *Economic Journal 93*: 763–82.

Weitzman, M. (1985). 'The Simple Macroeconomics of Profit Sharing'. *American Economic Review 75*: 937–53.

6 The role of central planning under capitalism and market socialism

Alec Nove

There is, in my view, much confusion about the role of planning, defined here as deliberate intervention with or substitution for market processes by public authorities, and the confusion extends all the way from the extreme Right (or neoliberals) to the extreme Left (or neo-Marxists). Perhaps the word 'central' may be too restrictive in this connection; some kinds of planning powers by public authorities may be exercised locally with reference to local needs.

A common feature of capitalism and 'market socialism' is that a large part of the economy is subject to the control and criteria of the market, at least so far as current operations are concerned. This is based on a number of presuppositions. One is that there is a *competitive* market and that the sector in question is appropriate for competition.

This does not, of course, mean anything resembling the 'perfect competition' of the textbook, since it is hardly ever met with in real life. It means simply that there are several suppliers of any particular good or service, that customers can choose, with knowledge, among alternative sources of supply and that the bargaining process includes price, quality, delivery dates, after-sales service and other relevant dimensions. External economies and diseconomies and indivisibilities may complicate this simple relationship, of course. In these instances, microprofitability may be a poor guide to general economic interest, in ways that we will explore in this chapter. There is also the question of natural monopolies, of which water supply is a vivid example. Water supply illustrates another principle, relevant to both kinds of economy: This could be called the public-service aspect. Thus apart from being a natural monopoly (it would be wasteful to duplicate the network of water pipes), the supply of clean water is rightly regarded as essential, and so its provision does not depend primarily on its profitability. (The market may help to identify the most economically effective way of achieving the desired objective, but the objective itself is decided on non-economic grounds.)

There could be, and often are, disputes as to where to draw the line between what could be called commercial as against public-service provision, as well as between what is charged for and what is 'provided free'. Housing, education, health, public transport, libraries are to various degrees seen as candidates for profit-orientated privatisation by neoliberal extremists. In Great Britain the telephone service has been privatised, despite being a rather evident case of a natural monopoly, and the post office is not safe from the 'neoliberal' fanatics – though they too can sometimes appreciate the difference between provision and responsibility. Thus to take another example, rubbish must be collected and public-hospital sheets washed; so far as I know, not even Milton Friedman would dispute this. But he would prefer that the responsible (public) authority hire subcontractors to carry out these tasks. Proposals whose authors take them seriously are put forward to privatise prisons. Here again, the idea is for the public authority to employ private enterprise, an idea that is by no means new: Prisoners have been rented to chain-gang operators, and while they are about it, why not privatise tax collection? 'Tax farming' has a long (if not particularly salubrious) lineage.

There will be much more to say on the subject of where the boundary lines of 'market' are, or should be, in modern capitalism, as well as in a real or imagined market socialism. However, there are other dimensions of great importance: One is investment and the capital market and the linked questions of regional development and environmental protection. The other is the whole question of 'macro' balance, the avoidance of mass unemployment, of extremes of cyclical fluctuations and finally (of great significance for any sort of socialism) of excessive income differentiation and unequal property ownership. The neoliberal extremists, believers in laissez faire, claim that the economy is basically self-equilibrating, that the market provides all or almost all the necessary signals, that 'markets clear' if various 'imperfections' (e.g., wage and price stickiness) are eliminated and that government 'macro' intervention is almost always harmful and/or unnecessary. This view is linked with 'monetarism', but there is no necessary connection: One can imagine a socialist and interventionist treasury still anxious to keep careful control over the money supply to avoid inflation. Surely most socialists, whether of the market or antimarket variety, would or should be conscious of the fact that markets and automatic economic forces cannot solve all problems.

6.1 Market, public provision and planning at 'micro' levels

'Micro' is here defined as including not only firms (enterprises) but also the provision of specific goods and services. Common sense as well as the Soviet experience strongly suggests the need to distinguish among sectors. Some are much more amenable to central planning than others. This can be due partly to economies of scale, partly to the location of the necessary information about needs and alternative sources of supply. The clearest example of a sector that is amenable to central planning is electricity generation and distribution. All major countries have an inter-connected electricity grid, and it would be absurd (even Mrs. Thatcher's advisers should see this!) to grant powers to the managers of every power station to generate electricity by reference to the profitability of their own power station taken in isolation. The element of *system* is strong. Furthermore, demand can be, indeed must be, assessed at the centre. Operational and economic criteria are best judged at that level, including the efficiency criteria applicable to specific generating stations.

Furthermore, since this is bound to be a monopoly and since any monopoly can improve its financial results at the customers' expense, price control becomes essential, as do some qualitative criteria (e.g., the avoidance of power cuts, the requirement to supply electricity to outly-ing areas, etc.). Also, investment decisions, involving addition to capac-ity, and choice between different forms of generation (gas, oil, coal, hydro) require the sort of information that is available only at the centre. This applies with equal force to capitalist and socialist economies. Market data, market prices, are, of course, an important element in deci-sion making but not, in this instance, a decisive one. Quantitative assess-ment of future demand and a view as to *future* relative costs and prices, requiring knowledge and judgment – these are decisive. There are, needless to say, no 'future markets' adequate for the purpose.

Many of the same considerations apply to other energy sources – for example, oil and gas, and probably coal too. Nor is it an accident that giant firms, many of them multinational, dominate steel, chemical, aero-space and computer production in most capitalist countries. In all these instances, major investment decisions are taken at levels far above the individual factory or plant. There are big economies of scale, a long ges-tation period and very large expenditures on research and development.

The 'textbook' advantages of competition are outweighed by the other considerations: the minimisation of uncertainty and risk, achieved through mergers, cartels and collusion. The 'Thatcher' ideology asserts that, nonetheless, private ownership is always preferable, because public enterprises cannot go bankrupt, that the capital they use is not risk capital. But in fact these very large private enterprises cannot be allowed to go bankrupt either, as can be seen with British Leyland or (in America) Chrysler.

Such very large industrial complexes are in fact centrally planned, to various degrees, in modern capitalism. Shell, Exxon and DuPont are hierarchically structured organisations of great size, dominated by a managerial bureaucracy. The separation of managerial power from ownership in these and many other instances has been commented on for more than a hundred years; Marx did not fail to notice it either. Yet both vulgar Marxists and vulgar neoclassicals persist in theorising 'as if' the capitalist entrepreneur of the traditional textbook were still typical. We shall return to the implications of this in a moment. Management, especially in America, is now highly mobile, owing no long-term allegiance to 'its' corporation. It is reported that the average American executive changes his firm in little more than five years. This, plus the great emphasis now placed on *short-term* profits as the key success criterion, plus inflationary and other uncertainties, places a big premium on decisions with a short time horizon. Overconcentration on the short term is also a 'disease' towards which Yugoslav 'self-management' is prone. This danger is worth emphasising.

Let us first turn to other sectors of the economy to which the 'straight' market criteria do not apply without very considerable modification. Transport facilities are a case in point. Thus most of the world (except Mrs. Thatcher's economic advisers) recognises that urban transport benefits those who do not use it (by reducing congestion and increasing property values), and that it should be provided by a public authority, with a sizeable subsidy to cover inevitable losses. Even in Reagan's United States, docks, airports and rapid-transit systems are publicly owned. Involved here are external economies (time saving, convenience) and diseconomies (congestion, pollution) and also elements of system, of network, which render the conventional marginal-cost and marginal-profitability analysis both misleading and irrelevant, and the public-service aspect of high importance. Of course, in making decisions one should always compare costs and results, but one can do so only in the context of the *network*, on the one hand, and the *purpose* of the activity, on the other.

The same applies, for example, to postal and telephone services. This used to be taken for granted even in the most capitalist of capitalist countries, but is so no longer, as can be seen by the privatisation of British telephones in 1984 and the breakup of the Bell telephone system (privately owned but seen as a *public* utility) in the United States. It was a *Labour* government in Britain that foolishly turned the Post Office from a government department into a 'commercial' corporation; so instead of being dominated by the public-service aspect, subject to financial constraints, it is now profit-orientated, subject to (minimal) public-service constraints, and there are now proposals to close rural post offices 'because they do not pay'.

Socialists, and most nonsocialists too, accept the public planning and provision of roads, street lighting, rubbish disposal, most education and fire services, though some of these can be subcontracted. I have already mentioned the fanatics who recommend privatisation of even prisons, and the London *Punch* printed a cartoon in which the management of the prison, facing losses, sells weekend passes to the richer prisoners. It is necessary to defend public housing programmes from the neoliberal ideologists and to do battle to save public health from profit-maximisers. The scandalously high costs of medical care in the United States can be cited as vivid evidence of what happens when the 'caring professions' become dominated by money making. One might have thought that even elementary neoclassical economics would have taught the 'Chicago' ideologists that there cannot be an 'efficient' market when the consumers, the patients, cannot possess needed information about the product and alternative treatments. Furthermore, basic principles are involved. It is quite reasonable to expect one's meat without the conscious beneficence of the butcher, bread without the beneficence of the baker, to cite Adam Smith's examples: They provide meat and bread out of a legitimate desire to make money. But if a doctor, faced with a sick child, inquires first into the income of the parents, then a society organised on such ethical principles seems to me to be under threat. For then why should judges and policemen also not seek to maximise *their* incomes?

To summarise this section of my analysis: There are important sectors in our economy that by reason of monopoly, size, the importance of externalities or the dominance of the public-service aspect, even under modern capitalism, are either publicly owned or in some important respect publicly regulated, or subsidised, or implicitly or explicitly guaranteed against bankruptcy. These are sectors that a 'market socialist' economy would place under state (in some cases local-government) control. There would, of course, be problems of efficiency criteria, responsibility and investment decisions. But these problems are not due primarily to the difference between public and private ownership. Also important is the question of self-management or worker participation, on the one hand, and the influence of the consumer-user, on the other. Precisely because, in these sectors, competition tends to be weak, absent or undesirable, the providers of the good or service may be able to abuse their power, and a management responsible to its own work force can 'exploit' the customer as well as any other. The state would thus require supervisory powers, and would as well have a major say in major investment decisions. The more so as, presumably, a market socialist economy would not have a stock exchange, and most of the capital required would come from the state banking system.

How large a segment of the entire economy would fall within the above categories? In real Western economies, side by side with public and private giants there are a vast number of small firms, and competition really does exist (though, needless to say, it is not 'perfect competition'). This is true of a very wide range of manufacturers (sometimes the necessary competition is provided by imports), construction, and service industries of many kinds. It is in these sectors, and also in agriculture, that the Soviet system tends to be least efficient, where central (or local) planning is stultifying, where efficiency criteria are apt to produce perverse results, results no one consciously desires (such as fulfilling plans in tons by wasting metal).

Distribution, trade, whether in means of production or in consumer goods and services, employs millions and is required to be subordinated to market criteria, to satisfying customer requirements and not to fulfilling plan instructions, which in these sectors are necessarily ambiguous and contradictory.

So here the market is indispensable, as are flexible prices, freedom to purchase inputs (and imports too) and so on. Here publicly owned firms must compete, with one another and with cooperative and private enterprise. Here too the extent of self-management may be limited only by the degree of interest in management questions on the part of the work force. They may prefer outside occupations and hobbies to sitting on committees. And we must learn from the negative aspects of Yugoslav experience about possible irrationalities in the behaviour of self-management enterprises; this is a subject I will not pursue here.

A possible danger worth mentioning is a well-intentioned fragmentation of those large units that, for technological or informational reasons, *ought* to be large. I myself quoted with approval the slogan 'small is beautiful'. But not at any cost. Yugoslav experience strongly suggests that fragmentation can go too far, can disintegrate what should be integrated. We can learn too from the muddled ideas of Mrs. Thatcher's privatisation ideologists, who have deliberately destroyed urban public-transport networks with different routes operated by separate private companies. This would be just as silly if bus routes were cooperative-owned. (Of course, *local* transport, serving the given locality, should be run by the local or regional public authority, not the centre.) Complementarity, indivisibility, can be important.

A left-wing critic of my ideas has expressed the fear that, in a socialist economy, separate autonomous enterprises might well make decisions that are inconsistent with the central plan.[1] Of course, they might. Since the partial and the general interests seldom coincide, such a danger is inherent in *any* form of decentralisation. True enough, cases could occur in which the centre's view is the correct one and should prevail. One must never forget, however, that the concentration of decision making at the centre is costly, both in terms of the needed collection and assessment of information and in bureaucratic delays and contradictions. One must try to identify in advance those sectors or types of decision making in which the centre may indeed know better. But these should be kept to the necessary minimum. An imagined optimal organisation chart should show a wide variety of decision-making powers at various levels. What is appropriate for large investments in steel or gas may be quite wrong if the decisions concern cabbages, trousers, pneumatic drills, electronic components, software, cafés or travel agencies. What *must* be wrong is any sort of mono-organisational model; variety is the spice of life.

6.2 The 'macro' level

One danger here, correctly noted by Frankel and also stressed by Tinbergen, is to imagine that a socialist market (or any other modern) economy can function smoothly without any central direction or steering at all. 'It is highly improbable that the proponents of a "laissez faire theory" of self-management are right. It can be convincingly shown that in an optimum order some tasks must be performed in a centralized way and cannot therefore be left to the lowest levels'.[2] Similarly, an interest-

[1]B. Frankel, *Radical Philosophy* (Spring 1985).
[2]J. Tinbergen, in B. Horvat R. Super, M. Markovic (eds.), *Self-governing Socialism: A Reader* (White Plains, N.Y.: Arts & Sciences Press, 1975), p. 226.

ing book devoted to a Spanish experience in self-management, by Thomas and Logan, argues that 'at the meso- and macro-levels, a strong planning agency is essential, as otherwise a self-managed economy could not function. Phenomena such as the entrance and exit of firms, and the adjustment process of capital intensity, can only be realized by careful planning and institutional support'.[3] Both these quotations are specifically related to problems of so-called self-management, but the reasons for the need for an economically active public authority remain, regardless of the internal arrangement of authority within the firm, so long as this unit does possess genuine autonomy in decision making. Evan Luard recently wrote a book entitled *Socialism without the State*, distancing himself from the unreal notion that the state can wither away. With the idea that state intervention should not be all-pervasive and stifling we can all agree. But then we should not fall for a socialist version of Chicago laissez faire economics. One such has been devised in Hungary by Tibor Liska. It is open to severe criticism.

Some of the necessary functions of the state in the economy have been sketched or implied in the previous few pages: big investment decisions, supervision of the large semimonopolist corporations, the definition and planning of 'public-service' and welfare sectors, including decisions about old age pensions, health and education. But more important in the present context is the realisation that the economy is not self-equilibrating, that markets do not necessarily clear, and this applies particularly to the labour market. Keynes does not cease to be right under market socialism. Freedom to respond to market signals can lead to overresponse, to booms and slumps, to failures and bankruptcies. Some critics rightly note that Soviet-type systems lack the economic discipline of the threat of bankruptcy (the 'soft budget constraint' of Kornai), but we must not extol bankruptcy as a 'good': When more than half of British and West German shipyards close, with the labour force idle, this is not quite what we mean by efficient utilisation of resources!

Many years ago, G. B. Richardson pointed to a contradiction in the formal neoclassical theory, for which perfect competition and perfect markets were an *optimum optimorum*, with reality treated as an imperfection.[4] Richardson pointed out that without so-called imperfect information and/or collusion no major investment would ever be made.

If the opportunity to invest profitably were perceived equally by all

[3]H. Thomas and C. Logan: *Mondragon* (London, Allen & Unwin 1982), p. 187.
[4]See his *Information and Investment* (New York: Oxford University Press, 1950).

potential competitors, there would be no profit for anyone and it would 'pay' no one to invest (alternatively, all would lose, achieving conspicuous waste). So the so-called imperfect, that is, partial, knowledge is in fact an essential precondition for action on the investment front. If this is so within a capitalist model, it is surely also important in a market socialist model too. Some naive believes in market automatism may be overreacting to the lesson to be drawn from bureaucratic overcentralisation.

It may be tempting to adopt a 'socialist-market-laissez-faire philosophy', and there were some who believed (believe?) that laissez faire would work better under socialism than it can under monopoly capitalism. I am convinced that this would be a grave error – just as it is plainly wrong to imagine that cyclical fluctuations could not happen within a centralised directive-planning system. (There is a sizeable literature on these fluctuations, among which T. Bauer's work is outstanding.) Of course, the causes would be different. However, laissez faire could well be expected to generate booms and slumps, requiring countercyclical 'Keynesian' intervention. Given a necessary commitment to near full employment, and given also that there is no assurance in the real world that 'labour markets will clear', the centre must assume responsibility both for undertaking (when necessary) job-creation activities and for so devising the rules under which autonomous enterprises function that they are not encouraged to adopt labour-saving techniques when there is serious unemployment; there are lessons to be learnt from the Yugoslav experience in this respect.

The whole question of investment, its purposes and indeed its aggregate magnitude, would surely be a major central-planning task in a market socialist economy. It is difficult to see how the 'time preference of the community' can be expressed other than by and through political organs. They too can and should determine some broad priorities: how much for housing, schools, hospitals. *Regional* policy would also affect the location of proposed investments. Some, no doubt, would be made on the initiative of enterprise management, so as to adjust productive capacity to anticipated demand, but central planners would have to draw on centrally controlled resources to set up new enterprises and to develop new kinds of technology. State credit institutions (investment banks) would play a key role, and among their tasks would be avoiding wasteful duplication and also reflecting the government's regional policies. (We know from the experience of many countries that unbalanced regional development tends to be cumulative rather than self-correcting.)

Should state credit institutions be numerous? Should they compete? If so, would not one effective indirect means of 'steering' the economy be gravely weakened? Or, to put the point another way, would the investment banks operate on normal commercial criteria, aiming at profits, or should their main task be to channel investment funds into enterprises and regions that conform to the state's planning priorities? Can the latter be combined with commercial criteria by differential tax or subsidy measures or even prohibitions (e.g., not allowing, or heavily taxing, any industrial investment in Mexico City, Budapest, Paris or similar overdeveloped regions)? It could also be argued that a state credit monopoly is undesirable, that a market economy requires the emergence of a capital market. This is one lesson that is said to have been learnt in Hungary. The state banking system was operated there with skill and flexibility, but is widely seen as insufficient. This can be viewed from several different aspects. First, enterprises with sizeable retained profits and reserves may well find that it is more rational to invest such sums in expanding some enterprise other than their own and should be encouraged to do so as and when the anticipated rate of return is higher. The same is true of any private or cooperative profits. At the same time, enterprise management would prefer a situation in which it can raise capital without necessarily applying for a credit from a (or the) state bank. In recent years Hungary has been trying out the marketing of bonds, carrying relatively high interest rates and a state guarantee, but issued (with permission) by enterprises.

These bonds are saleable, and their prices have been cited in the press. Some Hungarian economists (rightly!) deplore the state guarantee: This could be and should be *risk* capital. The bonds are not shares – they give no right to a voice in running the business – and some have suggested that, before long, issues of shares might also be authorised, though this seems unlikely. These bond issues are not a major source of capital at present, but their very existence establishes a precedent, a new principle for a country within the Soviet bloc. I mention it here because the Hungarian experience brings to the fore an important question: Can a 'socialist market economy' function effectively unless something resembling a capital market is also in existence? And what shape could such a market take in an economic system that can call itself socialist? These issues are now also in the area of public discussion in the Soviet Union.

Issues of employment and unemployment will surely be closely connected with incomes policies. Under full employment, the bargaining power of labour is strong. With militant trade unions pressing sectional claims, the stage would be set for 'leapfrogging' wage rises and to an ever increasing rate of inflation. As also in a capitalist economy today, inflationary uncertainties would distort economic decision making and give rise to familiar and highly undesirable phenomena. An incomes policy becomes an essential central responsibility. But this presupposes a consensus about the acceptable level of income inequality and also about differentials, and we know that these can be causes of serious conflict. Also, the operation of the market mechanism must inevitably generate substantial inequalities, especially in the presence of cooperative and even small-scale private enterprise. A tough progressive tax system would be needed to avoid (or minimise) what could be regarded as excessive and unreasonable income differentials, particularly between those doing work of similar skill and responsibility. There is a dilemma here: If success does not yield significantly higher incomes (and failure, lower incomes), there would be insufficient incentives, but if it does, the objectives of a socialist incomes policy may be frustrated and inflationary wage demands (and/or civil strife) could be the consequence. A delicate balancing act will be called for. This is now being debated in the USSR in the context of the 'Gorbachev' reform proposals.

There will also be discussions of 'socialist monetarism', since efforts have to be made to combat a tendency for personal incomes, credits and investment projects to exceed in aggregate the resources available. A democratic political structure would not make it any easier to cope with the pressures – on the contrary.

6.3 Some conclusions

Public authorities, at the centre and sometimes in localities, would have important functions to perform if 'market socialism' were to be adopted. Many of these functions in fact belong to the public authorities today in capitalist countries, and the efforts of the followers of the Chicago school (who surround Mrs. Thatcher) to 'privatise' and to rely on laissez faire are threatening political and social stability and are based (in my view) on inappropriate incrementalism, misplaced marginalism and myopic monetarism. *Because* socialists must be concerned with combatting unemployment, because total 'laissez faire' and socialism seem to me to be in principle incompatible, the role of the state and of planning should surely be substantial. It would indeed be necessary to avoid the centralised planning of current production and of material inputs, save in the few sectors (such as electricity) where even current production (of current!) is and should be amenable to central planning. The lessons of both the Soviet *(sovnarkhoz)* and Yugoslav experience also point to the danger of granting powers over industry to republic or provincial authorities, for this leads to the diversion of resources to the needs of these areas to the detriment of the wider interest. It is management responsive, through the market, to the variety of changing needs of customers that would be making most decisions most of the time. (I abstract here from the question of the relationship between management and the work force.) I have emphasised the importance of scale, and so also the level of management at which various decisions can or should be taken, as well as the role of the state in setting the ground rules for competition (and if competition is weak or undesirable in the given sector, public authorities may need to control prices and set performance standards).

It is necessary to repeat that responsibility for employment, incomes policy, the magnitude of accumulation and investment priorities, the avoidance of inflation and of booms and slumps will present to the central authorities of any market socialist society many challenges and perplexities. It presents many of these very same challenges to contemporary capitalist economies, and it would surely be quite unrealistic to envisage perfect socialist competition and perfect socialist markets whose automatic and smooth functioning would render central planning and state intervention unnecessary. And since 'the state' will inevitably consist of fallible human beings, subject to pressures from interest groups, under conditions that could include ecological and environmental crises and grave problems with (and in) raw-material-exporting countries, there may well be great difficulties in the way of maintaining economic and social balance.

Part II

Criteria

7 Are freedom and equality compatible?

G. A. Cohen

7.1 Self-ownership, world ownership and equality

Most right-wing philosophers believe that freedom and equality are conflicting ideals, so that if you have one of them, you cannot have the other
too. And they also believe that, when freedom and equality conflict,
freedom should be preferred and equality should be rejected. Some of
them regret that, as they suppose, equality has to be rejected, whereas
others see no harm in that.

Most leftists reply either that there is no real conflict between equality
and freedom, when both are properly conceived, or that, to the extent
that there indeed is one, freedom should give way to equality, since justice demands equality, and justice comes before all other political values.

This chapter is about equality and freedom, and its author is one kind
of leftist. But I shall not try to show that there is no conflict between freedom and equality for leftists to worry about. What I shall show, instead,
is that there is no conflict between what the Right *calls* freedom and
equality. The difficulty for socialists is not that we cannot preserve the
freedom that the Right offers and also promote equality. The difficulty is
that real freedom, which the Right cannot offer, may well require some
revision of the traditional Left egalitarian prospectus.

The right-wing conception of freedom is, I think, founded on the idea
that each person is, as one might put it, the *morally* rightful owner of
himself, even if existing legal systems do not fully acknowledge that

This chapter presents, in brief and unqualified form, the major contentions of two recent
publications: 'Self-Ownership, World-Ownership and Equality', in Frank S. Lucash (ed.),
Justice and Equality Here and Now (Ithaca, N.Y.: Cornell University Press, 1986), pp. 108–35;
and 'Self-Ownership, World-Ownership and Equality: Part II', in Ellen Frankel Paul, Fred
D. Miller, Jr., Jeffrey Paul, and John Ahrens (eds.), *Marxism and Liberalism* (Oxford:
Blackwell Publisher, 1986), pp. 77–96.

moral fact.[1] Let us call that the self-ownership thesis. The most impressive contemporary proponent of the self-ownership thesis is the Harvard philosopher Robert Nozick. He holds that each person possesses over himself, as a matter of moral right, all those rights that a slaveholder has over a complete chattel slave as a matter of legal right; and that each person is entitled, morally speaking, to dispose over himself in the way that such a slaveholder is entitled, legally speaking, to dispose over his slave. Such a slaveholder may not direct his slave to harm other people, but he is not legally obliged to place him at their disposal to the slightest degree: He owes none of his slave's service to anyone else. Analogously, if I am the moral owner of myself and, therefore, of my right arm, then, although others are entitled, because of *their* self-ownership, to prevent it from hitting them, no one is entitled, without my consent, to press it into their own or anyone else's service, even where my failure to lend it voluntarily to others would be morally wrong.

My failure to help someone could indeed, according to Nozick, be morally wrong, but he denies that anyone, be it a private person or the state, would then be justified in *forcing* me to help him. Notice, then, that Nozick does not encourage people not to help one another. Nor does he think that they should not be blamed if they never do so. What he forbids is *constrained* helping, such as is involved, or so he would claim, in redistributive taxation. No one, he thinks, enjoys an enforceable noncontractual claim on anyone else's service. The state must therefore refrain, for example, from taxing the rich person to pay for the poor person's medical care: Such taxation is a monstrous violation of the rich person's rights. But Nozick might nevertheless tell the rich person that it would be a jolly good thing if he contributed voluntarily to medical charity, and he might even say that a rich person who contributes nothing to charity is not at all nice. Nozick believes that people should be free to live their lives as they wish, but he does not believe that how they choose to live them is beyond criticism.

Nozick thinks not only that people own themselves, but also that they

---

[1] In so designating what is foundational and what is derivative in right-wing thought, I am suggesting that the right-wing idea is not that freedom comes first and, in order to be free, people should be self-owning. For the Right gives us no independent purchase on the concept of freedom that would enable us to tie freedom and self-ownership that way around. It is rather that the scope and nature of the freedom we must enjoy reflects the self-ownership conception. That is why the apparent unfreedom of the proletarian is not treated as a counterexample to the right-wing belief that freedom prevails in capitalist society. For the proletarian forced daily to sell his labour power is nevertheless a self-owner, indeed must be one in order to sell it, and is therefore nevertheless free in the relevant sense.

can become, with equally strong moral right, sovereign owners of the potentially indefinitely unequal amounts of worldly resources that they can gather to themselves as a result of proper exercises of their own and/or others' self-owned personal powers. When, moreover, private property in natural resources has been rightly generated, its morally privileged origin insulates it against expropriation of limitation.

Now a union of self-ownership and unequal distribution of worldly resources readily leads to indefinitely great inequality of private property in external goods of all kinds and, hence, to inequality of condition, on any view of what would constitute equality of condition. It follows that inequality of condition is, when properly generated, morally protected, and that the attempt to promote equality of condition at the expense of private property is an unacceptable violation of people's rights. Removing someone's legitimately acquired private property may not be as outrageous as removing his arm, but it is an outrage of the same kind. It is wrong for substantially the same reason.

A common left-wing response to Nozick is to recoil from the inequality his view allows, to affirm some sort of equality of condition as a fundamental principle, and to reject self-ownership because of the inequality of condition it supposedly generates. The left-wing conclusion is then that people lack the exclusive right to their own powers that goes with self-ownership, and that force may be applied against naturally well endowed people not only to prevent them from harming others but also to ensure that they help them, so that equality of condition (or not too much inequality of condition) will be secured.

But this line of response to Nozick, in which some sort of equality of condition is affirmed at the outset and a denial of self-ownership is derived from it, suffers from two related disadvantages. It has, first, the polemical disadvantage that the response is powerless against those who occupy Nozick's position, since they have not failed to notice that their view contradicts the fundamentalist egalitarianism that is here pressed against it. The other disadvantage of this response to Nozick is that the thesis of self-ownership has, after all, plenty of appeal on its own account, quite apart from anything Nozick says on its behalf. The antecedent appeal of the self-ownership principle rivals that of the egalitarian principles it is thought to contradict, even for many committed defenders of such principles: That, indeed, is why Nozick's book, *Anarchy, State and Utopia*, unsettles so many of its left liberal and socialist readers.[2]

---

[2]Robert Nozick, *Anarchy, State and Utopia* (New York: Basic, 1974).

In my experience, leftists who disparage Nozick's forthright affirmation of each person's rights over himself lose confidence in their unqualified denial of the thesis of self-ownership when they are asked to consider who has the right to decide what should happen to, for example, their own eyes. They do not immediately agree that, were eye transplants easy to achieve, it would then be acceptable for the state to conscribe potential eye donors into a lottery whose losers must yield an eye to beneficiaries who would otherwise be not one-eyed but blind. The fact that they do not deserve their good eyes, that they do not need two good eyes more than blind people need one and so forth – the fact, in a word, that they are merely lucky to have good eyes – does not always convince even left-wing people that their claim on their own eyes is no stronger that that of some unlucky blind person. But if standard leftist objections to inequality of resources, private property and ultimate condition are taken quite literally, then the fact that it is sheer luck that these (relatively) good eyes are mine should deprive me of special privileges in them.

Now one might infer, not that the usual objections to considerable inequality of private property in external things are without force, but that their force is due to the comparative antecedent weakness of the case for exclusive rights in *external* things. It is an intelligible presumption that I alone am entitled to decide about the use of this arm, and to benefit from its dexterity, simply because it is my arm. It seems not only as a mere matter of *fact* attached to me, but also something that, as a matter of *norm*, I *ought* to decide about the use of, and the same goes for these legs, this brain and all the other parts and faculties that are liable to be pressed into someone else's service. But there is no comparable presumptive normative tie between a person and any part or portion of the external world. Hence one may plausibly say of external things, or at any rate of external things in their initial state, of raw land and natural resources (out of which all unraw external things are, be it noted, made), that no person has, at least to begin with, a greater right in them than any other does; whereas the same thought is less compelling when it is applied to human parts and powers. Jean-Jacques Rousseau described the original formation of private property as a usurpation of what rightly should be held in common, and many have found that thesis persuasive. But few have discerned a comparable injustice in a person's insistence on sovereignty over his own being.

These reflections suggest that those who stand to the left of Nozick might consider a different reaction to him than from the one I described earlier. Instead of premissing that equality of condition is morally mandatory and rejecting self-ownership on that basis, they might relax their opposition to the idea of self-ownership but resist its use as the foundation of an argument that proceeds, via a legitimation of inequality in ownership of external resources, to defend the inequality of condition they oppose.

They might try to see whether, or to what extent, they can achieve the equality of condition they prize by adopting an egalitarian approach to worldly resources while accepting, or at any rate not rejecting, the thesis of self-ownership.

In the third section of this chapter I offer a critical assessment of one attempt to unite self-ownership with equality of worldly resources and preserve, thereby, equality of condition. But before embarking on that project, I shall show in the second section that, whatever may be said about the principle of self-ownership in its own right, and whether or not it can indeed by combined with equality of worldly resources, affirmation of it does not warrant the strongly inegalitarian distribution of worldly resources with which Nozick associates it.

7.2 Nozick on appropriation

Even now not everything around us is privately owned, and most people would think that what remains privately unowned, such as the air we breathe and the sidewalks we tread, should not be available for privatisation. But most of what we need to live by is, by now, private property. Why was its original privatisation not a theft of what rightly should be held in common?

Notice that the question applies not only to raw natural resources, but in fact to all private property in external things. For since people create nothing ex nihilo, all external private property either is, or was made of, something that was once no one's private property, either in fact or morally (or was made of something that was made of something that was once not private property, or was made of something that was made of something that was made of something that was once not private property, and so on). In the prehistory of anything that is now private property there was at least one moment at which something privately unowned was taken into private ownership. If, then, someone claims a Nozick-like right to something he legally owns, we may ask, apart from how he in particular came to own it, with what right it came to be *anyone's* private property in the first place.

Now it is easy to doubt that much actually existing private property was formed in what anyone could think was a legitimating way. Take for example, the shirt I am wearing. Superior force, nothing more, is the likely means whereby whoever first privatised the land from which came the cotton out of which it is made secured his title to it. But let us here set aside questions about actual history. Let us ask, instead, how, if at all, private property *could* legitimately be formed.

Nozick's answer to that question is that one may acquire 'a permanent bequeathable property right in a previously unowned thing' as long as 'the position of others no longer at liberty to use the thing is [not] thereby worsened'.[3] That is the condition he lays down for permissible initial appropriation. And it seems, on the face of it, a sufficiently stringent condition, which is to say stringent enough to ensure that, when the condition really is satisfied, no one can properly complain about the appropriation it endorses.

In a moment I shall show that that is an illusion, that Nozick's condition is in truth woefully lax. But first let me explain what the condition says. It requires of an appropriation of an object O, which was unowned and available to all, that its withdrawal from general use not make anyone's prospects worse than they would have been *had O remained in general use*. If no one's position is in any way made worse than it would have been had O remained unowned, then, of course, the condition is satisfied. But it is also satisfied when someone's position is in some relevant way worsened, as long as his position is in other ways sufficiently improved to counterbalance that worsening. Hence I appropriate something legitimately if and only if no one has any reason to prefer its remaining in general use, or whoever does have some reason to prefer that it remain gets something in the new situation that he did not have before and that is worth at least as much to him as what I have caused him to lose. To illustrate: I enclose the beach, which has been common land, declare it my own and announce a price of one dollar per person per day for the use of it (or, if you think that there could not be dollars in what sounds like a state-of-nature situation, imagine that my price is a certain amount of massage of my bad back). But I so enhance the recreational value of the beach (perhaps by dyeing the sand different attractive colors, or just by picking up the litter every night) that all would-be users of it regard a dollar (or a massage) for a day's use of it as a dollar well spent: They prefer a day at the beach as it now is in

[3]Ibid., p. 178

exchange for a dollar to a free day at the beach as it was and as it would have remained had no one appropriated it. Hence my appropriation of the beach satisfies Nozick's condition.

Now it might seem that appropriations satisfying Nozick's condition could not conceivably generate a grievance. But that, as I promised to show, is an illusion. It is possible for people to be made seriously worse off than they would have become, even when Nozick's condition on appropriation is fulfilled. For Nozick has arbitrarily narrowed the class of alternatives with which we are to compare what happens when an appropriation occurs with a view to determining whether anyone is harmed by it. One might agree with Nozick that the way to determine the legitimacy of an appropriation is by looking at what would otherwise have happened to the people concerned, but Nozick does not consider enough alternative possibilities.

To see this, imagine a world with two people, whom I shall call, for mnemonic reasons only, Grabber and Johnny-Come-Lately, or Johnny, for short. (Some people think it is unrealistic to draw morals from worlds with only two people in them, but everything I shall say about this small world can be applied to more realistic big ones.) Initially nothing is privately owned, and each lives on milk, which he gets by temporarily arresting lactating female wild moose and drawing it from them. Each spends an average of six hours per day doing that. Each thereby obtains a certain number of gallons of milk per year, a number that reflects the quality of his own moose-trapping and moose-milking powers, and who gets more milk is not here relevant. Now suppose that Grabber seizes all the land, and all the moose with it, and designs a division of labour under which he himself traps, for an hour each day, and Johnny milks, for six hours each day. What is more, Grabber offers Johnny a salary consisting of the same amount of milk per year as Johnny was able to get on his own. Grabber himself gets not only five extra hours of leisure but also much more milk from the new arrangement.

Then Johnny is not worse off than he was before Grabber's grab and, let us assume, than he would have become had the land and the moose *remained* unprivately owned. And this means that Grabber's appropriation is, by Nozick's condition, legitimate. He gains enormously in comparison with the state of nature, and Johnny gains nothing, but Johnny does not lose, so the privatisation is immune to Nozickian criticism.

Now to see that Grabber's appropriation is, though clearly legitimate according to Nozick, not clearly legitimate on a more searching view of the matter, consider these further possibilities.

1. Suppose Johnny is just as good an organizer as Grabber is. He could have done exactly what Grabber did, but he did not because he thought doing so would be too grasping. Then, although Grabber's appropriation satisfies Nozick's condition, it does not seem that Grabber has, what Nozick's condition gives him, the right to force Johnny to respect it.
2. That is more evident still if we now suppose that Johnny could have designed an even better division of labour than the one Grabber imposes under which *both* he *and* Grabber would have fared better than they do following Grabber's appropriation. Yet even under that supposition, Grabber's appropriation is, for Nozick, justified. It follows that Nozick's condition licenses, and protects, appropriations with upshots that make everyone worse off than he needs to be.
3. There is a third alternative with which to compare Grabber's appropriation, beyond the single alternative with which Nozick compares it, which is the persistence of unstructured common ownership, and the further alternative I complain he neglects, which is an appropriation by Johnny. That third alternative, also unjustifiably neglected by Nozick, is that it might be the case that Johnny and Grabber would have agreed to a division of labour without either of them privately appropriating the land. Such an agreement would, in effect, institute a form of socialism, and whether or not such a socialism would be productively superior to the dispensation following on one or other of the two private appropriations, it would certainly be productively superior to the initial no-ownership situation, and it is arbitrary to ignore how Johnny would have fared under the socialist alternative when considering whether Grabber's appropriation is justified.

Suppose, however, that Johnny lacks Grabber's organisational skills, that Grabber's appropriation actually makes Johnny better off than he was before and that socialism would, for some reason, benefit neither party by comparison with the initial no-ownership dispensation. Is not Grabber's appropriation, at least under those maximally favourable assumptions, as legitimate as Nozick thinks it is?

Note that, even if we say that it is legitimate, it is legitimate only by virtue of satisfying conditions far stronger than those Nozick lays down. And my own view is that its legitimacy is even then contestable. For to suppose otherwise is to take for granted that the land is not, from the start, collectively owned by Grabber and Johnny, so that the proper way to decide its fate would be by the socialist device of consensual agreement, instead of unilaterally. Why should we not regard the land, before Grabber's appropriation, as collectively owned rather than, as Nozick takes for granted, owned by no one?

Now the real-world equivalents of Johnny are those billions, a majority of humankind, who are born into the world substantially propertyless and who therefore depend for their survival on someone wanting to buy their labour power. What would Nozick say about them? He would say, of those propertyless persons who do manage to sell their labour power, that they will get at least as much and probably more in exchange for it than they could have hoped to get by applying it in an unregulated state of nature; and of those propertyless persons whose labour power is not worth buying that, though, in Nozick's nonwelfare state, they might therefore die, they would have died in the state of nature anyway.

But we can now make two replies to that tough and complacent talk about the lot of the dispossessed. The first is that, even if we concede that the world is originally, morally speaking, unowned, the fact that those now without worldly resources would have been no better off had the world remained unowned and not been privately appropriated in the particular way it was does not legitimate their condition, since it might be true that they would have been better off still if those private appropriations had not occurred. And the second reply is to withdraw the concession offered in the first one, by objecting that Nozick has not shown that the world's initial normative state *is* one of not being owned by anyone. What prevents us from regarding it as jointly owned to begin with, even if we also regard each of its inhabitants as a sovereign self-owner?

I conclude that we may dispatch Nozick's inegalitarianism without raising any challenge against the thesis of self-ownership.

7.3 Two concepts of liberty

What we may challenge is the blithe assumption that 'virgin' things are quite unowned and therefore up for grabs: One scarcely need share that assumption *even* if one accepts that people are full owners of themselves. Now one alternative to the view that things are, in their native state, quite unowned is, as we saw, to regard them as jointly or collectively owned by all persons, and I shall now present and discuss an attempt to combine that different conception of the original moral relationship between people and things with the principle of self-ownership, with a view to shedding some light on the distributive effect of self-ownership in a world whose parts are not open to unilateral privatisation. What follows is one attempt to realise the project described at the end of Section 7.1, the project of respecting self-ownership and subjecting worldly resources to an egalitarian dispensation, in the hope of securing equality of resultant condition without rejecting self-ownership.

Once again we imagine a two-person world, but once again the results will apply, mutatis mutandis, to a world teeming with people. This time our individuals are called Able and Infirm, after their respective natural endowments. Each owns himself and both jointly own everything else. With suitable external resources Able can produce life-sustaining and life-enhancing goods, but Infirm has no productive power at all. We suppose that each is rational and exclusively self-interested, and we ask what scheme of production and distribution they will agree on. We thereby investigate the reward that self-owned ability would command in one kind of world without private property.

Now what Able and Infirm get depends not only on their own powers and decisions but also on what the world is like, materially speaking. Five mutually exclusive and jointly exhaustive possible material situations, not all of which are interesting, may readily be distinguished:

1. Able cannot produce per day what is needed for one person for a day, so Able and Infirm both die.
2. Able can produce enough or more than enough for one person, but not enough for two. Infirm lets Able produce what he can, since only spite or envy would lead him not to. Able lives and Infirm dies.
3. Able can produce just enough to sustain both himself and Infirm. So Infirm forbids him to produce unless he produces that much. Able consequently does, and both live at subsistence.
4. If Able produces at all, the amount he produces is determined independently of his choice, and it exceeds what is needed to sustain both Able and Infirm. They therefore bargain over the distribution of a fixed surplus. The price of failure to agree (what theorists of bargaining call the 'threat point') is no production, and therefore death for both.
5. Again Able can produce a surplus, but now, more realistically, he can vary its size, so that Able and Infirm will bargain not only, as in situation 4, over who gets how much, but over how much will be produced.

The interesting cases are 4 and 5, in which bargains will be struck. It is a controversial question, in the relevant philosophical and technical literature, what one should expect the outcome of such bargaining to be. But it seems clear that the inputs to the bargaining process will be what are called the utility functions of Able and Infirm, including the disutility of labour for Able and the disutility of infirmity for Infirm. What will matter, in other and less technical words, is their preferences, what they like and dislike, and how much. And the crucial point is that Able's talent will not, just as such, affect how much he gets. If the exercise of his talent is irksome to him, then he will indeed get additional compensation, but only because he is irked, not because it is his labour that irks him. In short, he gets nothing extra just because it is he, and not Infirm, who does the producing. Infirm controls one necessary condition of production (relaxing his veto over use of the land), and Able controls two, but that gives Able no bargaining advantage. If a good costs 101 dollars and you have 100 of the needed dollars and I only one of them, then, if we are both rational and self-interested, you will not get a greater share of the good if we buy it jointly just because you supply so much more of what is required to obtain it.

Here, then, joint world ownership prevents self-ownership from generating an inequality to which egalitarians would object, and although the Able and Infirm story is an extremely special one in several respects, the particular point that talent as such yields no extra reward even under self-ownership, where there is also joint ownership of external resources, is, I believe, generalisable. (I do not say that no inequality repugnant to egalitarians can arise in the Able and Infirm situation, but only that either there will be no such inequality or its foundation will not be Able's ownership of his own powers but the parties' utility functions as they operate in the bargaining process. One cannot guarantee that no inequality repugnant to egalitarians will arise, since different egalitarians believe in different equalities, and not all of them are likely to emerge from the bargaining process.)

But we must now consider a seemingly fatal objection to the lesson just drawn from the Able and Infirm story. The lesson is that, without denying self-ownership and without affirming equality of condition as an underived principle, one may move towards a form of equality of condition by insisting on joint ownership of the external world. And the seemingly fatal objection is that to affirm joint ownership of the world is, as the story of Able and Infirm might be thought to show, inconsistent with achieving the purpose and expected effect of self-ownership. What is the point of my owning myself if I may do nothing without the agreement of others? Do not Able and Infirm jointly own not only the world but also, in effect, each other? Would they not bargain exactly as they do if we supposed that, instead of being self-owning, they jointly owned one another? It looks, then, as though the suggested form of external resource equality, namely, joint world ownership, renders nugatory the self-ownership with which we have sought to combine it. Self-ownership is not eliminated, but it is made useless, rather as it is useless to own a corkscrew when you are forbidden access to bottles of wine.

But the objection just stated can, for the present polemical purposes, be set aside. Joint world ownership indeed renders self-ownership merely formal, but, as we shall see, that is not an objection that defenders of capitalism are entitled to press.

The polemical task of the present chapter is to respond to Robert Nozick's contention that honouring people's self-ownership requires extending to them a freedom to live their own lives that is incompatible with the equality of condition prized by socialists. Our response to that contention was that self-ownership is, contrary to what Nozick says, compatible with equality of condition, since the inequality that Nozick defends depends on adjoining to self-ownership an inegalitarian principle of external resource distribution, which need not be accepted. When, instead, self-ownership is combined with joint ownership of the world, its tendency to generate inequality is removed.

The objection to that response was that the resource distribution under joint world ownership renders the self-ownership with which it is officially combined merely formal. *But that objection would, for immediate polemical purposes, be laid to rest if it could be shown that the self-ownership defended by Nozick is itself merely formal*, for he could not then maintain that what he defends generates inequality of condition.

To be sure, Nozick would like us to think, what he evidently himself thinks, that the self-ownership he favours is more than merely formal. In Chapter 3 of *Anarchy, State and Utopia* he pleads that each person should be free to live his own life, a *desideratum* that is supposed to be secured by the rights constituting Nozickian self-ownership. But Nozick also thinks that the most abject proletarian, who must either sell his labour power to a capitalist or die, enjoys the relevant rights. And if that is so, then Nozick could not complain that Able's self-ownership is merely formal, since, whether or not it is indeed merely formal, it is not less consequential than the proletarian's.

If Able and the proletarian lack substantive self-ownership, that is because neither can do anything without the agreement of Infirm and the capitalist, respectively. But they are, nevertheless, different from chattel slaves; for while each can do nothing without another's agreement, it is also true that there is nothing that either need do without his own agreement: Neither Infirm nor the capitalist has rights of sheer command that are not grounded in a prior contract to obey. By contrast, the slave's master may determine unilaterally what the slave must do.

The resulting dilemma for Nozick is severe. Either capitalism does not confer consequential self-ownership, since the worker's self-ownership is not robust enough to qualify as such, or, if it does so qualify, consequential self-ownership is at least as robust as the worker's, and no inequality follows from self-ownership in the world of Able and Infirm.

Let me describe Nozick's dilemma in a different way. He says that a propensity to inequality is unavoidable when people are allowed to live their own lives. Yet he must hold that, despite the constraints on his life choices, the proletarian leads his own life. But it then follows that he is wrong that, when people lead their own lives, equality of condition cannot be guaranteed, since Able and Infirm lead their own lives as much as the proletarian does, and the constitution under which they live guarantees a certain equality of condition.

We can now draw three conclusions. First, the tale of Able and Infirm shows that strict socialist equality is compatible with the freedom that defenders of capitalism boast everyone has in capitalist society, since that freedom is nothing more than formal self-ownership, and formal self-ownership obtains in the world of Able and Infirm.

Second, although it indeed turns out that the freedom of which Nozick speaks can be reconciled with equality, that is only because it is a very confined freedom, and it remains to be shown that equality can be reconciled with a freedom more worthy of the name.

Such freedom – and this is the third conclusion – is not self-ownership, but autonomy, the circumstance of genuine control over one's own life. Universal self-ownership fails to ensure autonomy, since it tends to produce proletarians, who lack it. Universal self-ownership does not produce proletarians when it is conjoined with appropriate rules about external resources, but such rules, to preserve self-ownership while securing everyone against proletarianhood, must breach autonomy in a different way. The indicated conclusion is that, for real freedom, or autonomy, to prevail, there have to be restrictions on self-ownership. That is ironical, since it is autonomy that attracts us to self-ownership, through a disastrous misidentification. The very thing that makes the self-ownership thesis attractive should actually make us reject self-ownership.

The natural next step is to ask what kind and degree of control over external things a person must have to enjoy autonomy, and then to ask whether such control is compatible with socialist equality. Those questions compose a real challenge to contemporary Left political philosophy, even after Nozick has been set aside. Nozick's freedom is consistent with equality, but the same may not be true of a freedom whose claims are less illusory. But I have to add, at the cost of ending on a pedantic instead of a rhetorical note, that I do mean just that there *may* be incompatibility between socialist equality and freedom. Whether there actually *is* that incompatibility is a matter for further investigation and debate.

8 Self-realisation in work and politics: the Marxist conception of the good life

Jon Elster

In arguments in support of capitalism, the following propositions are sometimes advanced or presupposed: (a) The best life for the individual is one of consumption, understood in a broad sense that includes aesthetic pleasures and entertainment as well as consumption of goods in the ordinary sense. (b) Consumption is to be valued because it promotes happiness or welfare, which is the ultimate good. (c) Since there are not enough opportunities for consumption to provide satiation for everybody, some principles of distributive justice must be chosen to decide who gets what. (d) The total to be distributed has first to be produced. What is produced depends, among other things, on the motivation and information of the producers. The theory of justice must take account of the fact that different principles of distribution have different effects on motivation and information. (e) Economic theory tells us that the motivational and informational consequences of private ownership of the means of production are superior to those of the various forms of collective ownerships.

In the traditional controversy over the relative merits of capitalism and economic systems, the focus has been on proposition (e). In this chapter I consider instead propositions (a) and (b). Before one can even begin to discuss how values are to be allocated, one must consider what they are – what it is that ought to be valued. I shall argue that at the center of Marxism is a specific conception of the good life as one of active self-realisation, rather than passive consumption.[1] It is a conception that, with various qualifications and modifications, I am also going to defend

This chapter is reprinted from *Social Philosophy and Policy* 3 (1986): 97–126, by permission of Bowling Green State University Press. I am grateful to my colleagues in the project 'Work and Social Justice' at the Institution for Social Research for their comments on earlier drafts of this chapter. Special thanks are due to Fredrik Engelstad for his guidance in the literature on work satisfaction.
[1]The broader interpretation of Marx that sustains this assertion is set forward in my *Making Sense of Marx* (Cambridge University Press, 1985).

by arguing that self-realisation is superior to consumption both on welfarist and on nonwelfarist grounds.[2]

It ought to be noted, before I proceed, that is is far from obvious that political theory ought to be concerned with determining the proper conception of the good life. John Rawls argues, for instance, that the goal of political philosophy is to determine the just distribution of 'primary goods', that is, the goods that everyone would want in order to realise his or her own conception of the good life.[3] It would be unjustified paternalism if the state were to intervene in order to promote a special conception of the good by influencing the availability of various options or trying to foster the desire for some rather than others.

I have much sympathy for this liberal argument. The idea that someone other than the persons concerned knows what is best for them has a long and unsavoury history whose lessons should not be forgotten. Yet liberalism is also and obviously incomplete, in that it neglects the *endogeneity of preferences*.[4] Liberalism advocates the free choice of life-style, but it forgets that the choice is to a large extent preempted by the social environment in which people grow up and live. These endogenously emerging preferences can well lead to choices whose ultimate outcome is avoidable ruin or misery.[5] Although this resistible preemption is vastly preferable to a dictatorially imposed conception of the good life, it casts a long shadow on the presumed sovereignty of individual preferences. The political question remains, however, even granting that people do not desire that which would be best for them, how, except in a dictatorial or paternalist fashion, could a change for the better come about? The solution must be a form of self-paternalism: If people do not want to have the preferences they have, they can take steps – individually or collectively – to change them.[6]

Hence the thrust of this chapter is twofold. Substantively, it argues for

[2]For the notion of welfarism, see Amartya Sen, 'Welfarism and Utilitarianism', *Journal of Philosophy* 76 (1979): 463–88.

[3]John Rawls, *A Theory of Justice* (Cambridge, Mass.: Harvard University Press, 1971), pp. 90–5. I ought to add that there is much in Rawls's book that goes beyond the simple consideration of primary goods. In particular, his discussion of what he calls the Aristotelian Principle (p. 424ff.) has many affinities with the present analysis of self-realisation. Yet his argument for the design of basic social institutions does not go beyond primary goods.

[4]See my *Sour Grapes* (Cambridge University Press, 1983), chap. 3, for the importance of endogenous preference formation in political philosophy.

[5]For an extreme example of how one can 'improve oneself to death', see Carl Christian von Weizsacker, 'Notes on Endogenous Change of Tastes', *Journal of Economic Theory* 3 (1971): 356.

[6]On the notion of individual and collective self-paternalism, see my *Ulysses and the Sirens*, rev. ed. (Cambridge University Press, 1984), chap. 2.

a certain conception of the good life. Methodologically, it argues that such substantive questions are not outside the scope of political theory. The structure of the argument is as follows. Section 8.1 exemplifies and defines the notion of self-realisation, argues for the superiority of self-realisation over consumption and tries to explain why people may nevertheless resist its attractions. The following sections discuss the two main vehicles of self-realisation that have been discussed in the Marxist and neo-Marxist tradition. Section 8.2 considers the concept of *work* and argues that, in spite of the apparent disutility of work, it can be a channel for self-realisation. Section 8.3 discusses the neo-Marxist idea that *politics* can provide an outlet for self-realisation, through participation in political discussions and decision making. Section 8.4 considers both of these vehicles in the light of the Marxist view that the value of self-realisation ought to be implemented jointly with that of *community*, that is self-realisation for others or with others. Section 8.5, finally, looks more closely at ways in which the desire or opportunity for self-realisation could be promoted or blocked by various institutional arrangements. I conclude with some tentative remarks on how to get from here to there.

8.1 The concept of self-realisation

8.1.1 Some examples and a preliminary classification
Here is a list of some activities that can lend themselves to self-realisation: playing tennis, playing piano, playing chess, making a table, cooking a meal, developing software for computers, constructing the Watts Towers,[7] juggling with a chain saw, acting as a human mannequin,[8] writing a book, contributing to the discussion in a political assembly, bargaining with an employer, trying to prove a mathematical theorem, working a lathe, fighting a battle, doing embroidery, organising a political campaign and building a boat.

Activities that for various reasons do not lend themselves well to self-realisation can be roughly divided into spontaneous interpersonal relations, consumption and drudgery. The first class of activities range from

---

[7]The Watts Towers in Los Angeles were constructed single-handedly by an Italian immigrant, Sam Rodia, over a period of thirty-three years, out of debris and bric-a-brac that he collected from the streets of the city. (For information see the *Los Angeles Times*, Aug. 12, 1984.) They are beautiful in conception and execution, unlike, say, conceptual art, which has mainly the freakish value of stunning novelty, soon fading into boredom. For a discussion of the conditions for self-realisation in art, see Elster, *Sour Grapes*, chap. 2, sec. 7.

[8]This example and the preceding one were observed at Venice Beach in Los Angeles. They are included to remind us that self-realisation is not always channelled into activities that in some substantive sense are socially useful.

talking with friends to making love; they do not lend themselves to self-realisation because they are not defined by some further goal or purpose. Consumption activities include eating a meal, reading a book or paying for the services of a prostitute; the reason they do not lend themselves to self-realisation is spelled out in detail below. Drudgery includes sweeping the streets, working on an assembly line or (with the qualifications discussed in Section 8.3) voting in an election; it does not lend itself to self-realisation because it very soon becomes trivial or boring.

These classes of activities can also be compared along the dimensions of *purposiveness* and *satisfaction*. In consumption, the purpose of the activity is to derive satisfaction. In self-realisation, the purpose is to achieve something, and satisfaction is supervenient upon the achievement rather than being the immediate purpose of the activity. Spontaneous interpersonal relations can be deeply satisfying but have no purpose beyond themselves. Drudgery has a well-defined purpose, but is inherently unsatisfying. One should add that the purpose of drudgery normally is to produce something that is satisfying, that is, a use-value. A final class of activities, therefore, would be those that are inherently unsatisfying and produce nothing or little that is of value. Punishment that took the form of digging ditches and filling them up again would be an example. Some forms of 'community work' for the unemployed also approach this category, in that the unemployed are set to do work that society normally does not value enough to pay for.

As these examples indicate, a particular kind of activity may not be confined to a single category. Raising children or having sexual relations, for example, can be drudgery under certain conditions, consumption under others, self-realisation under still different circumstances and spontaneous interaction in some cases. The central features that turn an activity into a potential vehicle for self-realisation are that it has an external goal and that it can be performed more or less well – that is, the goal can be realised to a higher or lower degree – according to independently given criteria. If an activity is to be an actual vehicle for self-realisation, its goal must be of suitable complexity – neither so simple as to produce boredom nor so difficult as to produce frustration. The activity must offer a *challenge that can be met*.

Although self-realisation can be deeply satisfying, the satisfaction must not be the immediate purpose of the activity. Self-realisation belongs to the general class of *states that are essentially by products,*[9] that

---

[9]For a general discussion of this notion, see Elster, *Sour Grapes*, chap. 2.

is, states that can come about only as the side effect of actions undertaken for some purpose, such as 'getting it right' or 'beating the opposition'. In Section 8.3, I discuss how the quest for self-realisation through political participation is self-defeating if the political system is not oriented towards substantive decision making. The same danger can arise in self-realisation through creative work, if the artist becomes too preoccupied with the process of creation itself.

The main argument of this chapter is built around the comparison between consumption and self-realisation in terms of their inherent benefits and disadvantages. This approach can be justly criticised as too narrow, since the choice between the two forms of activity ought also to be considered in terms of their impact on spontaneous interpersonal relations, which are an important part of the good life on most people's conception. On the one hand, for instance, the tendency for self-realisation to expand into all available time, because of the economies of scale that characterise it, is a threat both to consumption and to friendship. On the other hand, one could argue that friendships based on joint self-realisation are more rewarding than those that are rooted in common consumption. I am unable to assess the net effect of these opposed tendencies.

8.1.2 Towards a definition
In the Marxist tradition, self-realisation is the full and free actualisation and externalisation of the powers and the abilities of the individual. I shall discuss the four components of this definition in the order in which I have just mentioned them. The full motivation behind the definition will become clear only in Section 8.1.3, where the reasons for valuing self-realisation are set out.

The fullness of self-realisation. The idea that the individual can *fully* bring to actuality *all* the powers and abilities he possesses is one of the more utopian elements in Marx's thought and certainly not one that I am going to defend.[10] One is constrained to choose between being a jack-of-several-trades and a master of (at most) one. I shall argue that the latter option ought to be chosen, because of the economies of scale that characterise self-realisation. It is, however, an important question exactly how a 'trade' or skill is to be defined. I argue in Section 8.2 that self-realisation

---

[10]Well-known passages in which Marx insists on the fullness of self-realisation are found in *The German Ideology*, in K. Marx and F. Engels, *Collected Works* (London: Lawrence & Wishart, 1976), 5: 47, 394.

through work in a constantly changing society may require the development of general skills that can be harnessed to widely differing tasks.

The freedom of self-realisation. Even though an individual cannot develop *all* his abilities, he ought to be free to develop *any* of them. The notion that self-realisation must be free but cannot be full is captured in a 'putty-clay' model of human nature.[11] Ex ante the individual should be free to choose which of his many powers and abilities to develop, but ex post the roads he did not take become closed to him. The reason that the choice of a vehicle for self-realisation must be freely made by the individual is that otherwise it would not be *self*-realisation. The individual is both the designer and the raw material of the process. Hence self-realisation presupposes self-ownership, in the weak sense of the right to choose which of one's abilities to develop. If I want to write poetry but also have the potential to become a doctor or engineer, there could be no justification for society to force me – for example, by means of an ability tax – to choose one of the latter options. It would, however, be justified in creating incentives to channel my desire for self-realisation into socially desirable occupations, so long as I am not punished if I choose otherwise. Negative and positive incentives ought to be linked to the activities actually performed, not to potential activities.

Note, however, that self-realisation does not entail self-ownership in the stronger senses of (a) the right to choose when to deploy one's (trained) abilities or (b) the right to retain the full income one can derive from that deployment. It does not impinge on the doctor's self-realisation if he is forced to treat patients in a disaster area or to pay taxes on his income. One may or may not think that some of his other rights would be violated, but that is not the issue here.

The formal or negative freedom to choose any given line of self-realisation ought not to be confused with the positive freedom or opportunity to do so. If I want to realise myself by making epic technicolor films, I may be unable to do so because I lack the material resources, even if nobody actively tries to block my desire. A society cannot guarantee that all individuals will get what they need in order to carry out their preferred project of self-realisation, since it might then be impossible to match the demand for resources with the supply. It can, however, try to create a large variety of opportunities for self-realisation and good

[11]For this approach to production see Leif Johansen, 'Substitution versus Fixed Production Coefficients in the Theory of Production', *Econometrica* 27 (1959): 157–76.

mechanisms for matching desires with opportunities. In doing so, how- ever, it will be constrained by the need to favor (a) forms of self- realisation that do not require excessive amounts of material resources and (b) forms that lead to the creation of material resources.

Self-actualisation. I decompose the notion of self-realisation into self- actualisation and self-externalisation. Self-actualisation itself can be ana- lytically depicted as a two-stage process, although in reality the two stages proceed pari passu. The abilities and powers of the individual are two steps removed from actuality: They must first be developed and then be deployed. Being able to (learn to) speak French is a condition for knowing how to speak French, and this, in turn, is a condition for speaking French.[12] The actual deploymnent of the ability is, of course, the raison d'être for its development and that which gives value to self-realisation.

Self-externalisation. The individual has many powers and abilities which may be deployed in ways that cannot be observed by others. One may train one's ability to enjoy poetry or wine, but the use of this power is not a part of the public domain. It is consumption rather than self- realisation. One may, however, externalise the power by interpreting poetry for others or taking up the occupation of wine taster, in which case the activity becomes a potential vehicle for self-realisation. Enjoying wine is not an activity that can be performed more or less well, although one may enjoy the wine more or less. By contrast, professional wine tast- ing lends itself to evaluation by external criteria.

8.1.3 Why value self-realisation?
I shall argue that both the self-actualisation and the self-externalisation aspects of self-realisation provide reasons for desiring it. Both of these arguments are welfarist in character, the first directly and the second more indirectly. In addition, I shall argue that even under conditions in which the desire for self-realisation does not lead to increased satisfac- tion, it can be a desirable desire to have on grounds of autonomy.

The need for suspension of tranquillity. Leibniz wrote that 'l'inquiétude est

[12]For a conceptual analysis of abilities and their actualisation, see Anthony Kenny, *Action, Emotion and Will* (London: Routledge & Kegan Paul, 1963), chap. 8. Kenny's is an Aristotelian concept of self-actualisation, to be distinguished both from the Freudian notion of liberating one's repressed thoughts and desires and the Nietzschean one of identifying with one's deeds. For a useful discussion, see Alexander Nehamas, 'How One Becomes What One Is', *Philosophical Review* 92 (1983): 385–417.

essentielle à la félicité des créatures.[13] This premise also has a central place in Marx's argument for self-realisation:

It seems quite far from [Adam] Smith's mind that the individual, 'in his normal state of health, strength, activity, skill, facility', also needs a normal portion of work and of the suspension of tranquillity. Certainly, labor obtains its measure from the outside, through the aim to be attained and the obstacles to be over-come in attaining it. But Smith has no inkling that this overcoming of obstacles is in itself a liberating activity. [Labour] becomes attractive work, the individual's self-realisation, which in no way means that it becomes mere fun, mere amuse-ment, as Fourier, with grisette-like naiveté, conceives it. Really free working, e.g., composing, is at the same time precisely the most damned seriousness, the most intense exertion.[14]

The central intuition behind this passage can be stated in terms of the Solomon – Corbit theory of 'opponent process'.[15] A rough diagrammatic statement of their theory is provided in Figure 8.1, which allows us to compare the utility streams derived from episodes of (at least some types of) consumption and self-realisation. Let us first define an episode *AC* – of either kind – as the time from the beginning of the activity to the time when utility is back to the preactivity level. Any given consumption epi-sode, then, has the pattern that it is initially pleasurable, but includes painful withdrawal symptoms when the activity ceases. The 'main pro-cess' *AB* has the opposite sign of the 'opponent process' *BC*. Conversely, in self-realisation the main process is painful – 'Aller Anfang ist schwer' – and the payoff comes at the end of the episode. If we consider repeated episodes, of qualitatively the same kind, the theory postulates that the opponent process comes to dominate the main process. The pleasures of consumption tend to become jaded over time, while the withdrawal symptoms become increasingly more severe. The consumption activity remains attractive not because it provides pleasure, but because it offers release from the withdrawal symptoms.[16] Conversely, the attractions of

---

[13]*Nouveau essais sur l'Entendement Humain*, in G. W. Leibniz, *Die Philosophischen Schriften*, ed. C. J. Gerhardt, 7 vols. (Hildescheim: Olms, 1966 reprint), 6: 175.

[14]Marx, *Grundrisse* (Harmondsworth: Penguin Books, 1973), p. 611.

[15]Richard L. Solomon and J. D. Corbit, 'An Opponent-Process Theory of Motivation', *Psychological Review 81* (1974): 119–145. See also my 'Sadder but Wiser? Rationality and the Emotions', *Social Science Information 24* (1985): 375–406. For an application to the pres-ent problem, see Frank J. Landy, 'An Opponent-process Theory of Job Satisfaction', *Journal of Applied Psychology 63* (1978): 533–47.

[16]It might be objected that this is a model of addictive consumption, not of consumption generally. With nonaddictive consumption, one cannot assume an increasingly strong opponent process, although the idea of decreasing strength of the main process remains plausible. Since the latter is all I need for my argument, it is not affected by the objection. In any case, there may be an element of addiction (in the sense of an increasingly strong opponent process) in all forms of consumption, although it is usually less dramatic than in the use of drugs, tobacco and alcohol. The objection might then be rephrased as a ques-

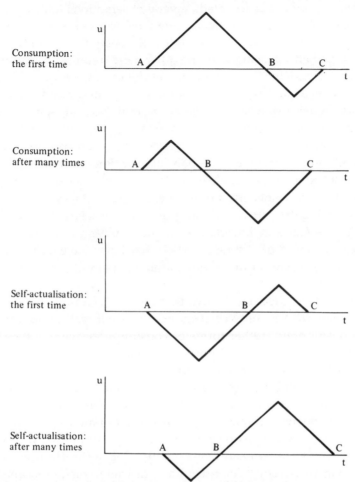

Fig. 8.1. Temporal patterns of utility corresponding to single episodes of consumption or self-actualisation, at early and later stages.

self-realisation increase over time, as the start-up costs diminish and the gratification from achievement becomes more profound.[17] There are economies of scale in self-realisation, whereas consumption has the converse property.

tion about whether the net effect of a given episode always becomes negative as the number of episodes increases.

[17]There are two exceptions to this statement. First, some abilities might not be susceptible to indefinite development; second, some persons might not be able to develop their abilities indefinitely. Tic-tac-toe, unlike chess, soon becomes boring; a person with poor motor reflexes might find out the hard way that he was not made for chain saw juggling. Economies of scale obtain only if abilities and tasks are suitably matched so as to avoid either of the extremes of boredom and frustration.

If this rough model is accepted, several observations follow. First, to derive maximal benefit from consumption, one should search for variety and diversity in order to enjoy the high initial benefits from many different activities. Self-realisation, on the other hand, requires concentration on one line of activity in order to exploit the economies of scale. Since variety soon becomes expensive, people with limited means (i.e., most people) do better if they choose self-realisation. Second, self-realisation has the pattern of 'one step backwards, two steps forwards', both within and across episodes. The initial stage *AB* of any given episode is always painful, although it becomes less painful over time. Moreover, the first times the net effect of the whole episode *AC* may be negative, while episodes with a positive net effect only emerge at later stages. Many people find that writing their first article for publication is a largely painful process, with a small and uncertain element of pleasure. At later career stages, the net effect of writing an article may be positive, but even then usually on the condition that the beginning is painful.

The self and others. I asserted above that there is a contrast between the temporal patterns of utility corresponding to self-realisation and *some types of* consumption. Other forms of consumption, namely those that represent self-actualisation without self-externalisation, exhibit the pattern of the bottom diagrams of Figure 8.1. Learning to read poetry, for instance, is a painful process; the payoff comes later. Moreover, on any given occasion there are start-up costs that may deter one from picking up a book of poetry, so that instead one turns to a crime novel. Some forms of consumption essentially involve deferred gratification. The similarity between such consumption activities and self-realisation will be obvious to many parents. The reason it is difficult to make children take, say, piano lessons is exactly the same as the reason it is hard to persuade them to read the first fifty pages of a book that, one feels sure, will then capture their interest. The culprit in both cases is myopia, that is, resistance to delayed gratification.

To explain why self-realisation ranks above such forms of self-actualising consumption, I shall invoke a Hegelian argument.[18] The most important value for human beings is self-esteem. Self-esteem derives largely from the esteem accorded one by other people. Esteem requires something that can be esteemed, some form of externalisation of one's

---

[18]See G. W. F. Hegel, *Phenomenology of Spirit* (New York: Oxford University Press, 1977), pp. 118, 193, 395–7.

inner self. It is of no avail to be a 'beautiful soul' if the soul remains ineffable and mute; the self must be made part of the public domain. This argument is closely linked to the need for external criteria of evaluation. Other people perform the indispensable function of assessing, criticising and praising one's performance; they provide the 'reality control' without which self-actualisation would be like a 'private language,' a morass of subjectivity. (I return to this issue in Section 8.4.2.)

Drudgery can also be a form of self-externalisation that provides esteem and, hence, self-esteem. The fact that one does or produces something that someone is willing to pay for shows that one is being useful and not a burden on others, even when the task itself is inherently uninteresting. This is only indirectly a welfarist argument. It would be simplistic to say that self-esteem is a source of welfare, happiness or utility. It is, more fundamentally, a condition for the ability to derive welfare from anything. Self-esteem is needed for the motivation to go on with the business of living. When we say that a depressed person suffers from low self-esteem, we mean that it is the cause of the suffering, not its object.

Self-realisation and autonomy. In Section 8.5 I argue that the lack of desire for self-realisation may be due to 'adaptive preferences', that is, to the adjustment of desires to what is possible. In a society with few opportunities for self-realisation, it may *for that reason* not be highly valued. With more opportunities, the desire might emerge. Yet we ought to consider the possibility that increased opportunities for self-realisation might generate more desires than can be satisfied.[19] If so, the increase in opportunities might make people on the whole worse off in terms of welfare, and yet we might want to say on nonwelfarist grounds that the change was a good thing. For reasons of autonomy, it is better to desire things because they are desirable than to do so because they are available. Many people would agree with this if one used freedom rather than self-actualisation as an example, but the argument applies no less to the latter case. To bring the point home, consider an example used by Ronald Dworkin in his rebuttal of welfarist conceptions of equality.[20] Imagine a gifted artist or scientist who, despite his great achievements, is desperately unhappy because he is acutely aware of his shortcomings. Indeed, it is precisely because of his great gifts that he, more than others, can per-

---

[19]For a more detailed exposition of a similar argument, see Elster, *Sour Grapes*, pp. 124, 133–40.
[20]Ronald Dworkin, 'What Is Equality? Part 1: Equality of Welfare', *Philosophy and Public Affairs* 10 (1981): 222.

ceive how far his achievement falls short of the ideal. When the circle of light expands, so does the surrounding circle of darkness. It would be simplistic to say that this person should go into another occupation, where he can set his sights lower and not think of himself as a fraud. The achievements of such people are inseparable from their total dedication to what they are doing. Although the darkness makes them depressed, they cannot live without the light. Theirs are lives worth living, though not on grounds of welfare.

8.1.4 Resistance to self-realisation

Yet there are other reasons, beyond adaptive preferences, that people might not desire self-realisation. Even when there are available opportunities, people might not take them because of myopia, risk aversion or free riding.

Myopia. The fact that self-realisation involves deferred gratification, both within and across episodes, must enter importantly into the explanation of why it is not chosen even when its superiority is clearly recognised. As I have argued elsewhere,[21] this is not simply a question of time discounting. It can also, more centrally, be a question of weakness of the will. People may desire a life of self-realisation and take the first, relatively costless steps towards it, and yet not bring themselves to undergo the painful learning process that is required.

Risk aversion. I have emphasised that self-realisation requires a matching of abilities and tasks to avoid boredom and frustration. It is not, however, a question of choosing a task that is optimally suited to given and known abilities. The situation, unfortunately, is one in which one of William Blake's Proverbs of Hell finds ample application: 'You never know what is enough unless you know what is more than enough'. The only way for the individual to find the limits of his abilities is, often, to come up against them.

To model the problem decision-theoretically, let us assume that the individual confronts the following situation:

	Task	
Ability	Easy	Complex
High	30	100
Low	50	10

[21]'Weakness of Will and the Free-Rider Problem', *Economics and Philosophy* 1 (1985): 231–65.

The numbers indicate the satisfaction that the individual derives under the different combinations of ability level and task complexity. They assume that matching ability and skill is always preferable to nonmatching, that high-level matching is better than low-level matching and that the frustration from having chosen a task that is too difficult is worse than the boredom from having chosen one that is too easy. Let us first assume that the choice involves risk with, say, equal probability that one's ability will be high or low. A risk-neutral individual would choose the complex task, but a risk-averse one might well choose the easy task. Next, assume that the situation is totally clouded in uncertainty, so that no probabilities can be assigned to the various ability levels. In that case, many people would use the maximin strategy of choosing the task that guarantees the highest minimal satisfaction, which again is the easy task. In either case, the conclusion follows that people individually might be deterred from choosing the course of action that would make them better off on the average. In theory, risk pooling could overcome the problem, but it is hard to see how any viable insurance system could be set up.

Free riding. It must be emphasised that if risk aversion makes people eschew the more demanding vehicles for self-realisation, they do not in any way act irrationally. The need for security is not an objectionable one. Yet before we conclude that risk aversion is an insuperable obstacle to self-realisation, we must consider another aspect of the problem. Self-realisation is not only rewarding for the individual who engages in it. It also provides gratification for those who consume the output of the activity. To the extent that people choose to realise themselves by engaging in scientific or technological activities, they produce medicines that save lives and innovations that make available to everybody and at low cost products that formerly were reserved for an elite. Even those whose efforts at self-realisation are frustrated because they overestimated the level of their ability benefit from the activities of those who correctly estimated their ability to be high.

This shows that self-realisation is also a problem of collective action. It is probably better *for everybody*, and not just on the average, if all act as if they were risk neutral, even if they are risk averse. Yet for each individual, it is always tempting to be a free rider and benefit from the risk taking of others, while acting in a risk-averse manner. To overcome the free-rider problem, self-realisation would probably have to become a social norm, although various other solutions are also possible.[22]

I add two further remarks on this problem. First, it is not clear that even risk-neutral behaviour would bring about the socially desirable outcome if the subjective probabilities are correctly formed. Either risk loving or overestimation of one's own abilities may be required. The following passage from a book by two cognitive psychologists is well worth reflecting upon:

People sometimes may require overly optimistic or overly pessimistic subjective probabilities to goad them into effective action or prevent them from taking dangerous action. Thus it is far from clear that a bride or groom would be well advised to believe, on their wedding day, that the probability of their divorce is as high as .40. A baseball player with a batting average of .200 may not be best served, as he steps up to bat, by the belief that the probability that he will get a hit is only .2. The social benefits of individually erroneous subjective probabilities may be great even when the individual pays a high price for the error. We probably would have few novelists, actors or scientists if all potential aspirants to these careers took action based in a normatively justified probability of success. We also might have few new products, new medical procedures, new political movements, or new scientific theories.[23]

Second, we may use this occasion to dwell on the distinction between the self-realisation of men and that of Man.[24] It is part and parcel of the ethical individualism of Marxism (further discussed in Section 8.4) that communism ought not to be justified by the prospects of great achievements for Mankind, but by what it offers to each and every individual. It is characteristic of class societies that they allow for the self-realisation of Man at the expense of that of most individuals, by enabling scientific and cultural achievements by the few at the expense of the drudgery of the many, while communism in Marx's conception will allow the full and free self-realisation of *each individual*. We can retain both the ethical individualism of Marx and the emphasis on self-realisation without accepting this utopian conception. The revised version of the ideal is the free and partial self-realisation of some, as a result of the attempted self-realisation of all, justified by the fact that the benefits of success also accrue to those who fail in the attempt.

[22]For a survey of ways in which free riding can be overcome, see the article; cited in the previous note and also my 'Rationality, Morality and Collective Action', *Ethics 96* (1985): 136–55.

[23]Richard E. Nisbett and Lee Ross, *Human Inference: Strategies and Shortcomings of Social Judgement* (Englewood Cliffs, N.J.: Prentice-Hall, 1980), p. 271.

[24]For this distinction, see G. A. Cohen, 'Karl Marx's Dialectic of Labour', *Philosophy and Public Affairs 3* (1974): 235–61.

8.2 Work as a vehicle for self-realisation

The main tradition in economic thought has looked at work as largely unpleasant, justified only by what it produces.[25] Marx, as we saw in the passage from the *Grundrisse* cited earlier, had a different view. Although he dissociated himself from Fourier's view that work could be made into 'mere amusement', he also took exception to Adam Smith's view that work was, necessarily, 'a curse'. Work, according to Marx, is rewarding *and* painful; moreover, it cannot be rewarding without being painful.

Contemporary industrial psychologists have also, from a very different perspective, considered the intrinsic benefits of work. They have almost exclusively discussed the comparative benefits and hardships associated with different forms of work, without asking themselves whether and when work is preferable to its absence, even if income is kept constant. This focus is understandable, whether the concern is with empirical testing or industrial reform, since the option of gaining a full income while not working is not feasible. Yet, from the present perspective, this option can enter usefully into various thought experiments designed to bring out the distinction between motivation and welfare – between what people prefer to do and what is best for them. I argue first that, for several reasons – one of which is self-realisation – people may be better off working even if they would prefer not to. I then consider the extent to which the argument from self-realisation applies to industrial work in modern societies.

8.2.1 The 'disutility of work'

The very definition of work constitutes a problem. I shall use the term in a broad and somewhat loose sense, to refer to any organised and regular activity whose purpose is to produce use-values or intermediate goods for the production of use-values. It is sometimes made part of the definition of work that it involves some pain or cost, even if only opportunity costs, to the worker. For reasons to be made clear, I do not follow this usage. Nor is it essential for the definition that work be remunerated.

Why do people work? Serge Kolm has offered the following list of reasons.

Because of direct coercion, as in forced labor
In exchange for a wage

[25]For a full survey, see Ugo Pagano, *Work and Welfare in Economic Theory* (Oxford: Blackwell Publisher, 1984).

Because of a desire to help and serve others
Out of a sense of duty or reciprocity
Out of interest for the work itself
For the sake of social relations at the work place
To show others that one is making a contribution to society or that one
   possesses certain skills
Because of the social status associated with work
To escape boredom
As play
Out of habit[26]

The notion of the disutility of work may be considered in the light of some of these reasons for working. Independently of the income from work, a person is usually made worse off by never working than by holding a regular job. Yet given the choice of whether to work or to abstain, with the same income, he might prefer to abstain. This may also be true even if it is rephrased in marginalist terms. For all n, it may be true that, if given a choice between working n hours per week and working $n - 1$ hours, a person would always prefer the latter option, yet would be worse off from never working than from working a full week. This situation arises because the person neglects the positive externalities of work or, what amounts to the same, the negative externalities of unemployment. These externalities are not effects on other people, but on the person himself at later times. The situation is an intrapersonal, intertemporal Prisoner's Dilemma.[27]

To understand the precise character of the externality, consider the work place as a source of friendship and self-esteem. For any n, a reduction in working hours from n to $n - 1$ will have little immediate impact on these benefits. A person would not lose his friends or their esteem by working slightly less, and he would gain some leisure. He might well prefer the reduction. Yet the cumulative long-term damage to his social life may be more substantial and outweigh the short-term gain in leisure. Each hour he is absent from work creates negative externalities for future periods, by loosening his insertion in the web of social relations and reducing his sense of his own worth.

A similar argument applies to the benefits derived from work as self-realisation. As I made clear towards the end of Section 8.1, myopia can

[26]S. C. Kolm, *La bonne economie* (Paris: Presses Universitairs de France, 1984), pp. 119–20.
[27]For discussion, see Elster, 'Weakness or Will'.

be a major cause of resistance to self-actualisation. Hence the 'marginal utility of work' would have a very different value if it were measured at the beginning of a given task and again when the task approached completion.[28] Even if one considered the marginal utility of the task as a whole, the value would depend heavily on whether one considered an earlier or a later performance. I conclude that the marginalist approach to the utility of work is ill-conceived, since work tasks are not made up of homogeneous bits, but have a complex temporal structure.

8.2.2 The scope for self-realisation in industry

Can work in modern societies provide a mode of self-realisation? Marx usually cites art and science as paradigms for self-realisation, which is not very helpful. Even though he insisted that communism would be based on large-scale industry and argued against conceiving of work on the model of the artisan, his examples of self-realisation fit the latter better than the former. Recent work in industrial psychology is more useful, although it does not, for several reasons, fit my purposes perfectly. For one thing, it takes for granted the property relations and incentive structures of capitalist firms; for another, the central concept of 'job satisfaction' is much broader and vaguer than the concept of self-realisation (as it is used here).[29] Reasons of space and competence prevent me from trying to summarise these studies here, but I shall try to restate and discuss some of the findings in terms of the framework set out in Section 8.1.

A recent survey lists work, pay, promotion, verbal recognition and working conditions as the main causes of job satisfaction. The first of these is further specified in terms that are quite close to my present approach:

Work attributes that have been found to be related to work interest and satisfaction include: opportunity to use one's valued skills and abilities; opportunity for new learning; creativity; variety; difficulty; amount of work; responsibility; non-arbitrary pressure for performance; control over work methods and work pace (autonomy); job enrichment (which involves increasing responsibility and con-

---

[28]In some cases, it would also give a different result if measured very close to completion; consider Byron's 'Nothing so difficult as a beginning / In poesy, unless perhaps the end'.

[29]In the literature on job satisfaction the notion of self-realisation is usually discussed with reference to the writings of Abraham Maslow and dismissed as hopelessly confused. See, for instance, Edwin A. Locke, 'Nature and Causes of Job Satisfaction', in Marvin D. Dunnette (ed.), *Handbook of Industrial and Organizational Psychology* (Chicago: Rand McNally, 1976), pp. 1307–9. Although I agree with the criticism of Maslow, I hope that the present discussion shows that the notion is not inherently unamenable to precise analysis.

trol); and complexity. While each of the above factors is conceptually distinguishable from the others, there is one element which they share in common, the element of *mental challenge*.[30]

Similarly, one influential writer argues that

work redesign can help individuals regain the chance to experience the kick that comes from doing a job well, and it can encourage them to once more *care* about their work and about developing the competence to do it even better. These payoffs from work redesign go well beyond simple job satisfaction. Cows grazing in the field may be satisfied, and employees in organizations can be made just as satisfied by paying them well, by keeping the bosses off their backs, by putting them in pleasant rooms with pleasant people, and by arranging things so that the days pass without undue stress or strain. The kind of satisfaction at issue here is different. It is a satisfaction that develops only when individuals are stretching and growing as human beings, increasing their sense of competence and self-worth.

He further decomposes the conditions for job enrichment into five elements: skill variety, task identity, task significance, autonomy and feedback.[31] Clearly, this is a pie that can be cut many ways. There seem to be, nevertheless, some common assumptions and problems that can be related to my concerns here.

Routine, variety or complexity? Monotonous, repetitive tasks, by and large, are not conductive to job satisfaction. Monotony can be alleviated by increasing either task variety or task complexity. Increasing task variety can take the form of job rotation in semiautonomous groups, but there seems to be some scepticism about this solution.[32] In terms of the framework used here, the scepticism can be justified by observing that job rotation does not permit one to exploit the economies of scale of self-realisation. Variety is a desideratum in consumption, not in work. True, it is better to rotate between several simple tasks than to devote oneself full time to one of them, but full-time concentration on one complex task is better still.

J. Richard Hackman argues, however, that 'not all jobs are suited to all people. Some individuals prosper in simple, routinized work, while others prefer highly complex and challenging tasks. . . . What percentage of the workforce actually desire higher order need satisfaction and so are

---

[30]Locke, ibid., p. 1319.

[31]J. Richard Hackman, 'Work Design', in J. Richard Hackman and J. Lloyd Suttle (eds.), *Improving Life at Work* (Santa Monica, Calif.: Goodyear, 1977), pp. 96–162.

[32]Gordon E. O'Brien, 'The Centrality of Skill-Utilization for Job Design, in K. D. Duncan, Michael M. Gruneberg and Donald Wallis (eds.), *Changes in Working Live* (New York: Wiley, 1980), p. 180. See also Hackman, 'Work design', pp. 115–20.

likely to respond to enriched jobs? Some observers estimate that only about 15 percent of rank-and-file employees are so motivated'.[33] From the argument in Section 8.1, two objections to these statements follow immediately. First, instead of saying that some people like challenges and others do not, one should say that what *is* a challenge differs across people. Second, the fact that many people do not desire challenging work does not mean that they would not 'prosper' in it, once they got over the initial hurdles.

Matching workers with jobs. G. E. O'Brien distinguishes among several strategies for achieving this match.[34] First, one can adapt the tasks to the workers by reform at the work place. This strategy has the most central place in the literature. O'Brien raises the question of whether economic democracy could be geared to this purpose. In his opinion, this will not be a successful strategy, for the reason, among others, that 'the less skill-utilization and influence people have in their jobs, the more likely it is that they see their lives as being determined by others. . . . This expectation makes it difficult for them to respond initially to changes in jobs or power structures which provide them with more autonomy'. I return to some aspects of this problem in Section 8.5.1.

Conversely, one may try to fit the worker to the task by suitable hiring criteria. According to O'Brien, 'Selection psychologists have done well in rejecting applicants with below required skill levels but have been less careful about rejecting applicants whose skill repertoire exceeds the job descriptions'. If it is correct, this observation could be explained by the fact that a capitalist firm has no incentive – or may not think it has an incentive – to avoid hiring overqualified workers. If an underqualified worker is hired, both the firm and the worker suffer, but only the worker suffers if he is overqualified.[35]

One may also attack the problem by long-term strategies of planning rather than short-term strategies of adaptation. One of these is to design new factories and organisations so as to facilitate the matching of workers and tasks. The other is 'to promote an educational policy which encourages students to have a realistic assessment of their own abilities and the probability of obtaining jobs which match these abilities'. The

---

[33]Hackman, 'Work design', pp. 115–20.
[34]O'Brien, 'The Centrality of Skill-Utilization', pp. 180ff.
[35]Hackman, 'Work design', p. 117, argues that overqualification also causes loss of productivity via the lack of motivation. This may well be true for some workers and some tasks, but sometimes a higher level of qualification probably leads to superior performance.

idea is presumably that with a more realistic assessment, students will decide not to develop abilities the deployment of which will meet no demand. The argument may or may not be valid, depending on the further assumptions made about individual motivation.[36] In any case, one must distinguish between two problems. As I mentioned earlier, no society can provide a guarantee that there will be a demand for a given ability. On the other hand, a good society ought to ensure that for each individual there is some ability he can develop that will meet an effective demand.

Autonomy and feedback. These requirements from the literature on job satisfaction reflect the interaction between the self and others in self-realisation. On the one hand, the task, to be satisfying, must be freely chosen and performed. 'An employee will not automatically like a task simply because it is challenging or because he has mastered it. He also has to like it for its own sake. This means that a man must choose the line of work *because he likes it*, not because someone else told him to like it, or because he is trying to prove something'.[37] On the other hand, the individual needs the recognition and evaluation of competent others, both to know how well he is performing and to give substance to his self-esteem. The most satisfactory feedback is provided by co-workers and clients rather than supervisors, since the latter are paid to use profitability rather than quality as the criterion for evaluating work.

The last observation points to a possible conflict between economic efficiency and self-realisation. Tocqueville recounts in *Democracy in America* that he 'met an American sailor and asked him why his country's ships are made so that they will not last long. He answered offhand that the art of navigation was making such quick progress that even the best of boats would be almost useless if it lasted more than a few years'.[38] With rapid technical change, the careful attention to detail that characterises most forms of self-realisation is pointless; conversely, pride

---

[36]Raymond Boudon, *Effets pervers et ordre social* (Paris: Presses Universitaires de France, 1977), chap. 4, argues that this can turn into a problem of collective action: It may be individually rational for each student to seek higher education, although all would be better off if all flipped a coin to decide. This presupposes, however, that students are motivated by expected income rather than by expected satisfaction, which would also take account of the disappointment and frustration generated by getting a low-education job at the end of higher education. Boudon himself (ibid., chap. 5) has the best treatment of this problem, although, surprisingly, he does not bring his analysis to bear on the problem of educational choice.

[37]Locke, 'Nature and Causes', pp. 1320–1.

[38]Alexis de Tocqueville, *Democracy in America* (New York: Anchor Books, 1969), p. 453.

in craftmanship may block innovation. The way out of this dilemma would have to be in the development of *adaptable skills* that can be harnessed to a variety of concrete tasks and, in fact, be enhanced by such variety. This would differ from job rotation in that each task would be an application and extension of the *same skill*, so that the economies of scale would not be lost.

8.3 Politics as a vehicle for self-realisation

Marx did not believe that there would be room or need for conflictual politics in communism; *a fortiori* he could not promote politics as a channel for individual self-realisation. Later Marxists have thought differently, notably Jürgen Habermas. He suggests that Marx overemphasised *work* at the expense of *interaction*, both in his theory of history and in his philosophical anthropology. The development of moral competence through rational discussion is a form of self-realisation that ought to be valued as highly as self-realisation at the work place.[39]

Since I have discussed this claim at some length elsewhere,[40] the present discussion will be more summary. On the one hand, politics may be conceived either as a *private* activity, or as one that essentially takes place in the *public* domain. On the other hand, it may be valued either as a *means to some nonpolitical end* or as an *end in itself*. The latter distinction is not an exclusive one: Politics may be valued both as a means and as an end. Indeed, the thrust of my argument is that to be an end in itself, it must also be a means to something beyond itself.

8.3.1 Private politics
According to this conception – memorably stated by Anthony Downs – the essential and almost only mass political activity is that of voting.[41] In Section 8.1 voting was classified as drudgery, that is, as inherently unrewarding, to be valued only for the outcome it produces. This characterisation hides a paradox, however, since it is hard to see how the outcome – an infinitesimally small chance of casting the decisive or pivotal vote – could motivate the act of voting (assuming that it is not compulsory).[42] Where the secret ballot is used, it is not plausible to argue that

[39]Jürgen Habermas, *Theorie des kommunikaliven Handelus* (Frankfurt aM: Suhrkamp, 1981).
[40]In my 'The Market and the Forum', in Aanund Hylland and Jon Elster (eds.), *Foundations of Social Choice Theory* (Cambridge University Press, 1986), pp. 103–32; see also Elster, *Sour Grapes*, chap. 2, sec. 9.
[41]Anthony Downs, *An Economic Theory of Democracy* (New York: Harper, 1957).
[42]See notably Brian M. Barry, *Economists, Sociologists and Democracy*, rev. ed. (University of Chicago Press, 1979).

voting has any consumption value.[43] Nor does it offer any scope for self-realisation, since it is not something that can be done more or less well. True, the decision to vote for one party or candidate rather than another may be the outcome of a process of deliberation that can be evaluated according to independent criteria, but to expose oneself to such evaluation is already to take leave of private politics. It is hard to see how voting could be anything else than drudgery, but equally hard to see what motivation it could have as drudgery.

The solution to the paradox is found in a class of motivations that include duty, fairness, internalised social norms and sheer magical thinking.[44] These attitudes are not easily categorized along the dimensions of purposiveness and satisfaction introduced in Section 8.1. Voting, under normal conditions, cannot be justified by any purpose and does not produce any satisfaction – except that of doing what one believes one ought to do. Then we must ask, however, why one should believe one ought to do something that neither has an extrinsic purpose nor produces intrinsic satisfaction. I am not going to pursue this question here, except to note again that behaviour guided by duty or social norms is somewhat recalcitrant to the conceptual scheme used here.

8.3.2 A controversy over ancient politics

The argument that politics is mainly or even exclusively to be valued as a form of self-realisation has been put forward in discussions of the ancient *polis*. Hannah Arendt, especially, championed the view that politics in the ancient city-states was about the agonistic display of excellence and individuality, and nothing else: 'Without mastering the necessities of life in the household, neither life nor the "good life" is possible, but politics is never for the sake of life. As far as the members of the *polis* are concerned, household life exists for the sake of the "good life" in the *polis'*.[45] In plain language, economics is a condition for politics, but not the object of politics. Nor, as far as one can glean from her text, did ancient politics have any other goal that could lend it value as a vehicle for self-realisation.

A more ironic version of Hannah Arendt's argument is provided by

---

[43]For a brief discussion and rejection of this possibility, see Howard Margolis, *Selfishness, Altruism and Rationality* (Cambridge University Press, 1982), p. 86.

[44]For further discussion, see chap. 5 of my *Cement of Society* (Cambridge University Press, 1989). More instrumental attitudes, such as altruist and utilitarian motivations, might also enter into the explanation of voting, but I believe that their importance is smaller than the ones mentioned in the text.

[45]Hannah Arendt, *The Human Condition* (University of Chicago Press, 1958), p. 37.

Stephen Holmes, who, when summarising the views of Benjamin Constant on ancient politics, also appears to deny that ancient politics had any nonpolitical end: 'Participatory self-government in the *polis* . . . was an improvised solution to the hoplite's awful problem: a surfeit of leisure time and the terrifying threat of ennui'.[46] The goal – escape from boredom rather than self-realisation – is more lowly, but the denial of any instrumental value to politics equally explicit.

This view may be challenged on factual grounds, as well as on grounds of consistency. For the first, we may look to the work of Moses Finley. He turns Arendt's view around and argues that 'in the city-states the premise, one might say the axiom, was widespread that the good life (however that was conceived) was possibly only in the *polis*; that the regime was expected to promote the good life; that therefore correct political judgments, the choice between conflicting policies within a *polis*, or, if matters reached such a stage, the choice between *polis* regimes, should be determined by which alternative helped advance the good life. . . . The good life, it should be stressed, had a substantial material component'.[47] Elsewhere, asking why the Athenian people claimed the right of every citizen to speak and make proposals in the Assembly, yet left the exercise of the right to a few, he finds that 'one part of the answer is that the *demos* recognized the instrumental role of political rights and were more concerned in the end with substantive decisions, were content with their power to select, dismiss and punish their leaders'.[48]

My claim is that of these two assertions – most people did not value politics as a vehicle for self-realisation; they did value politics as a means to nonpolitical ends – the second would be true even if the first were not. It is inconsistent to value political participation if it is not *about* something. It follows from the argument in Section 8.1 that political discussion must have an independently defined goal if it is to provide an outlet for self-realisation. The goal must be to make good decisions about what must ultimately be nonpolitical matters. To arrive at a good decision, political discussion must be guided by the norms of rationality; hence the powers and abilities brought to actuality by discussion are those of

[46]Stephen Holmes, *Benjamin Constant and the Making of Modern Liberalism* (New Haven, Conn.: Yale University Press, 1984), p. 60.
[47]Moses I. Finley, 'Authority and Legitimacy in the Classical City-State', *Det Kongelige Danske Videnskapernes Selskab. Historisk-Filosofiske Meddelelser 50*, no. 3 (Kobenhavn: Munksgaard 1982): 12.
[48]Moses I. Finley, 'The Freedom of the Citizen in the Ancient Greek World', in his *Economy and Society in Ancient Greece* (London: Chatto & Windus, 1981), p. 83.

rational deliberation. The more urgent and important the decision to be made, the greater the potential for self-realisation.

It follows that ancient politics as conceived by Arendt or Constant would be self-defeating. To escape boredom, one must be motivated by some other goal than that of escaping it. What is also – and somewhat inconsistently – emphasised by Holmes and Constant, however, is that the constant threat of *war* provided the indispensable, externally given object of ancient politics. The urgency of war concentrates the mind wonderfully and lends to politics the proper degree of seriousness without which it could neither be a remedy for boredom nor provide a vehicle for self-realisation.

Mass political participation, then, can be a form of self-realisation, if it takes the form of rational public discussion and decision making about substantive matters. National politics in modern societies involves too many people to provide an occasion for participatory self-realisation, while mass demonstrations and similar activities suffer from not being oriented towards decision making. The most promising arenas for this form of self-realisation are local government, economic democracy and democracy within organisations more generally. The conditions under which they lend themselves to self-realisation are further discussed in the next sections.

8.4 Self-realisation and community

According to Hegel and Marx, precapitalist societies were characterised by community without individuality. The modern period, conversely, has seen the emergence of frenetic individuality and the widespread disintegration of community. Marx believed that communism would bring about a synthesis of the two values. Although I cannot argue in any detail for this view here, I believe that his conception was inspired by the philosophy of Leibniz, who argued in a similar vein both that each monad differs from all others and that each monad reflects all others from its point of view.[49] On the one hand, people will tend to choose vehicles of self-realisation that correspond to their 'individual essences', to use a phrase from Leibniz. 'Milton produced *Paradise Lost* for the same reason that a silkworm produces silk. It was an activity of *his* nature'.[50] The ethical individualism of Marxism requires that 'above all we must

[49]Cf. my 'Marx et Leibniz', *Review Philosophique* 108 (1983): 167–77.
[50]Marx, *Theories of Surplus-Value* (London: Lawrence & Wishart, 1963), 1: 401.

avoid postulating 'society' again as an abstraction *vis-à-vis* the individual'.[51] On the other hand, the self-realisation of the individual must not be an agonistic and antagonistic process, but should take place in and for the sake of the community. According to Marx, self-realisation is integrated with community when it is *production for others*. I shall first consider this idea and then the alternative proposal that the two values might be reconciled in *production with others*.

8.4.1 Self-realisation for others

This ideal is most clearly stated in a passage from Marx's early manuscripts:

Let us suppose that we had carried out production as human beings. Each of us would have *in two ways affirmed* himself and the other person. (1) In my *production* I would have objectified my *individuality*, its *specific* character, and therefore obtained not only an individual *manifestation of my life* during the activity, but also when looking at the object I would have the individual pleasure of knowing my personality to be *objective, visible to the senses* and hence a power *beyond all doubt*. (2) In your enjoyment or use of my product I would have the direct enjoyment both of being conscious of having satisfied a *human* need by my work, that is, of having objectified *man's* essential nature, and of having thus created an object corresponding to another *man's* essential nature. . . . Our products would be so many mirrors in which we saw reflected our essential nature.[52]

The text is not transparently clear. It may, perhaps, be read as suggesting a distinction between two ways in which the appreciation of other people enhances the satisfaction I derive from work. On the one hand, I may derive pleasure from the pleasure they derive from my product. This will be the case only when I produce for people I know well, for example, when I cook a meal for my family. The idea that one can derive pleasure from knowing that one provides a service to 'society' is, in my opinion, unrealistic.[53] On the other hand, the critical assessment of other people is needed to tell me whether I am performing well or not. For this purpose, it is crucial that the assessment could be – and sometimes is – negative; 'sans la liberté de blamer il n'y a pas d'éloge flatteur'. Family members and friends cannot easily perform this function, since spontaneous interpersonal relations do not go well with this coolly evaluative attitude. Cooking

---

[51]*Economic and Philosophical Manuscripts,* in Marx and Engels, *Collected Works,* 3: 299.
[52]'Comments on James Mill', in ibid., pp. 227–8.
[53]The idea is central in Kolm, *La bonne economie*. Although Kolm is right in arguing that such 'general reciprocity' would overcome some of the defects of ordinary reciprocity, it would also lose the main virtue of the latter, namely, the warmth and spontaneity of personal relations.

for strangers is more satisfactory. Hence I suggest that Marx was wrong *if* he intended to suggest – but it is far from certain that he did – that one and the same reference group could perform both functions.

Even if cooking is drudgery rather than self-realisation, one might prefer to cook for strangers. Doing or producing something that others are willing to pay for is a source of self-esteem even when the work itself is not challenging or interesting. This may be among the reasons why women often feel the need to escape the close and sometimes suffocatingly ambiguous atmosphere of the family. To repeat, it is not a question of deriving pleasure from the fact that one does something which is socially valued, but of creating the conditions for deriving pleasure from other activities.

8.4.2 Self-realisation with others

An alternative synthesis of self-realisation and community would be producing *with* others rather than *for* them. It would be embodied in the work collective rather than in the producer–consumer community. I do not have in mind what one could call *common* self-realisation, in which each of several people would perform separate tasks under shared conditions. (Think of a group of scholars working together in a library.) Rather, I refer to *joint* self-realisation, in which 'the free development of each is the condition for the free development of all'.[54] (Think of the players in an orchestra or the participants in a political discussion.) Following the discussion in Sections 8.2 and 8.3, we may distinguish between joint self-realisation in work and in decision making. (The players in an orchestra, in addition to playing together, may also decide together which pieces to play and what to do with the proceeds from the concert.)

Consider, first, joint self-realisation in the production process. Historically, the trend in the division of labour has been towards greater integration and independence of tasks, on the one hand, and ever-simpler tasks with reduced scope for self-realisation, on the other. The mode of interdependence in modern industry is such that, if A does not do his job, B cannot do his – but it need not be true that the better A does his job, the better B can do his, and certainly not that B's good performance conversely enhances the conditions for A's good performance. And even if this is also the case, it need not be true that both tasks offer indefinite scope for improvement and growth. The conditions for joint self-

[54]*Manifesto of the Communist Party*, in Marx and Engels, *Collected Works*, 6: 506.

realisation may be observed on a small fishing vessel or in joint author- ship, but do not seem to be favored by the nature of industrial work.

Consider, next, participatory democracy at the work place. The first question that arises is that of efficiency. It is trivial to observe that any implementation of direct economic democracy would have to strike a compromise between the values of participatory self-realisation and effi- ciency. A similar compromise might have to be struck between self- realisation in work and efficiency, and in general between any two values one might want to promote. A less trivial statement is that participatory self-realisation may actually depend on efficiency. As argued above, the value of participation depends on the degree to which the object of partic- ipation is to make good decisions. In the present case, the goal is not to find the decision that would be best if found costlessly, but to make the best decision all things considered, *including the cost of decision making itself.* If enterprises run by direct democracy make a mess of it, the workers will get the benefits neither from efficiency nor from self-realisation. Hence maximal self-realisation occurs with a less than maximal degree of partic- ipation; total direct democracy would be self-defeating.

The market is a device for telling firms how well they perform. Hence an argument for market socialism, as distinct from state socialism, is that the threat of bankruptcy, like the threat of war, concentrates the mind wonderfully. I would like to illustrate this argument with a piece of per- sonal history. Around 1970, I was somewhat involved with two work collectives, a publishing firm that depended on market success for sur- vival and an academic institution that did not. Although the participa- tory democracy was much more strenuous and demanding in the first, it was also more rewarding. We gained much insight into the various subprocesses of publishing, and the way they came together in the final product: a book that is bought by someone. After a time, however, strain took its toll and the collective abdicated for a leader. In the second group, the lack of an independent goal and of well-defined performance criteria led to make-believe democracy. Discussion about who had the right to vote on what issues took up an increasing amount of time. The process of self-government turned inwards upon itself, with boredom rather than self-realisation as the predictable result.

We may contrast direct participatory democracy with representative economic democracy. Direct democracy is strenuous but rewarding, pro- vided that the efficiency constraint is respected. Representative democ- racy retains the virtue of justice, but does not provide scope for self- realisation for the rank and file of workers. The worst system is that which exists when direct democracy degenerates into activist rule, because too many people think the strains of participation exceed the rewards. Activists are not subject to the normal low-cost checks and controls of representative systems, only to the high-cost control of coparticipation.

There are two possible ways of coping with the instability of participatory democracy. One is to base the direct democracy on compulsory participation. My view is that, unless it is chosen unanimously as a form of collective self-control, reflecting the fact that self-realisation is strenuous and subject to weakness of will, this system would be unjustifiable. It would involve using other people as a means to one's own self-realisation and undermine the essentially free nature of rational discussion. The other solution is to have automatic transformation from direct to representative democracy when the level of participation drops below a certain level. If the activists are people for whom decision making is a central form of self-realisation, they could offer themselves as candidates in the representative elections. If they simply like untrammelled power, they would not thus offer themselves, which is as it should be.

These remarks apply to political democracy no less than to economic democracy. Under suitable conditions, both can be arenas for joint self-realisation. Although in economic democracy the collectivity is one of workers rather than of citizens, it is not oriented toward self-realisation in the actual work, but to self-realisation in the process of making work-related decisions. This does not mean that the workers perform managerial functions. They engage in a rational, knowledgeable discussion that issues in instructions to the managers. Managers may achieve self-realisation individually, by developing and deploying their administrative skills. The self-realisation of the workers would, like that of the musicians in an orchestra, be a genuinely joint one. If some of the participants deviate from the rules of a rational discussion, they thereby make it difficult or pointless for others to follow them.[55]

8.5 Institutions, desires and opportunities

What are the institutional conditions that could promote or block self-realisation? More precisely, how are the desire and the opportunity for self-realisation in work and politics affected by institutional relations within and between firms? This is a question that involves two inde-

[55]Habermas, *Theorie des kommunikativen Handelns*; see also Knut Midgaard, 'On the Significance of Language and a Richer Concept of Rationality', in Leif Lewin and Evert Vedung (eds.), *Politics as Rational Action* (Dordrecht: Reidel, 1980), pp. 87–93.

pendent variables and four dependent ones, and in addition we may expect there to be relations between the dependent variables. Here I shall only speculate about some of the connections that may obtain. I first raise the issue of adaptive preferences, already broached in Section 8.1. I then consider how relations within the firm may affect the opportunity for self-realisation and how relations between firms may affect both the desire and the opportunity. I conclude with some comments on 'how to get from here to there'.

8.5.1 Adaptive preferences
The absence of self-realisation may be due to the absence of a desire for self-realisation or to the absence of opportunities. If, in a given society, we observe that there are few opportunities for self-realisation and that people do not much seem to want it, it would be tempting to explain the first of these facts by the second. The causal chain could, however, go the other way. Because most people have few opportunities for self-realisation, their desires and aspirations might unconsciously adjust to this limitation, to avoid cognitive dissonance. In particular, a high rate of time discounting and a high degree of risk aversion might emerge endogenously, to make the best elements in the feasible set appear to be optimal even within the wider set that includes opportunities for self-realisation as well as for consumption. The idea that self-realisation is too strenuous and demanding may be tainted by an element of 'sour grapes'.[56] On the other hand, it may well reflect a respectable, autonomous preference for a quiet life or a life devoted to friendship. We would be able to tell the difference if more opportunities for self-realisation were available, for if they were still not chosen, it would show that the desire for a different life-style was an autonomous one, or at least one not shaped by the feasible set.

8.5.2 Democracy and size
Oliver Williamson and others have argued that there are inherent advantages of hierarchy over peer group organisation.[57] Hierarchy economises on the costs of diffusion of information, which is channelled through the leadership instead of being exchanged between all members in pairwise

[56]For a more detailed exposition of this argument, I again refer to chap. 3 of my *Sour Grapes*.
[57]Oliver E. Williamson, *Markets and Hierarchies* (New York: Free Press, 1975). For a recent survey, see M. McPherson, 'Efficiency and Liberty in the Productive Enterprise: Recent Work in the Economics of Work Organization', *Philosophy and Public Affairs* 12 (1983): 354–68.

interactions. It imposes a solution on trivial allocation problems that might otherwise have been the object of protracted bargaining. It is more consistent with the monitoring of labour productivity which, although not impossible in the peer group, violates its spirit. These advantages, finally, increase more than proportionally with the size of the group.

To assess these claims, the problem must be stated more precisely. I am concerned with evaluating economic institutions in terms of justice, the scope allowed for self-realisation and psychological stability. Efficiency is not explicitly an issue, but it enters indirectly as a requirement for self-realisation, as I argued above. Recall, moreover, that the peer group is supposed only to make major policy decisions, not to supervise the day-to-day activities of all members. It appears to me that all the advantages of hierarchy cited above could be preserved by having some members of the peer group perform managerial functions in accordance with these policy decisions. The difficulty, it would seem, arises at the level of these decisions themselves. Direct democracy is vulnerable to attrition and to plain lack of interest in decision making, for example, if the workers are fully engaged in self-realisation through work. Moreover, with large numbers of workers, it is technically inefficient and hence self-defeating *on its own terms*. To preserve efficiency and economic justice, delegation of decision making to elected representatives then becomes necessary. This arrangement would allow self-realisation for these representatives, but not for the rank and file. In the best of all possible worlds, the latter would then be able to achieve self-realisation in the work process itself.

Firm size depends largely on technology. To the extent that it is possible to channel technical change in the direction of smaller productive units, it is most urgent to do so in firms where the productive tasks themselves do not offer much scope for self-realisation. Because of the economies of scale in self-realisation, it is less important to insist on direct democracy where the work itself already offers sufficient challenge. Musicians in an orchestra may well prefer a dictatorial leader, even if he sometimes makes decisions with which they disagree, since this leaves them with more time to concentrate on their work.

8.5.3 Market or planning?
The macroeconomic institutions of a society will have a profound influence on both the desire and the opportunity for self-realisation. What I shall have to say about the impact on desires will be largely speculative, but I believe the comments on opportunities are somewhat more robust.

Central planning is not favourable to the two modes of self-realisation under discussion. To imagine participatory economic democracy in a centrally planned economy is almost a logical contradiction, since it would involve having the same decisions made by two different sets of people. (Imagine, moreover, the complications that would follow from participatory democracy in the planning agencies!) I have also argued that the market performs a useful function for self-realisation through work by providing independent external criteria of evaluation, whereas Soviet-type economies have been plagued by the difficulty of finding similarly nonmanipulable criteria. On the other hand, the 'market mentality' might work against self-realisation by providing incentives to produce profitable junk rather than high-quality products that meet no effective demand. The problem is analogous to the conflict between technical change and self-realisation mentioned above, and the solution would also have to be similar: to offer scope for self-realisation through general skills of tinkering and improvising.

'Market socialism' with direct economic democracy might also be thought to be, if not a contradiction in terms, at least psychologically unstable. Will not the competition among enterprises be incompatible with the solidarity within the enterprise that is needed to make self-management work? The role of solidarity is twofold. One the one hand, all workers must be motivated to work steadily without shirking. On the other hand, the more qualified workers must accept that the salary gap cannot be too large, that is, that the labour market must be regulated, since otherwise the motivation of the less qualified might be impaired. I do not know of any evidence that these requirements are incompatible with the spirit of competition. Without going so far as to say that solidarity cannot work unless it is solidarity *against others*, it appears to be a fact of life that intergroup competition and intergroup solidarity often coexist stably.

8.5.4 How to get from here to there (and remain there)
Consider some possibilities:

Workers under socialism prefer	Workers under capitalism prefer	
	Capitalism	Socialism
Capitalism	(i)	(ii)
Socialism	(iii)	(iv)

Scenario (i) corresponds to a dominant capitalist ideology: Workers do not want to move to socialism, and if they got there they would want to leave it. Scenario (ii) can be seen as an expression of 'counteradaptive preferences', created by the fact that both capitalism and socialism have many unattractive and ugly features, so that each of them would generate a desire for its opposite.[58] Scenario (iii) need not similarly be an expression of adaptive preferences. If socialism retains all the options of capitalism, while adding that of self-realisation, the desire in socialism for socialism would not be an adaptive one. The preference for capitalism in capitalism would, however, be adaptive. Scenario (iv) would seem totally utopian in the light of recent history. Note, however, that from the observed resistance to moving towards socialism one cannot infer a lack of preference for socialism, since the former might also be due to the costs of transition and the free-rider problem in revolutionary action.

I argued in Section 8.1 that the resistance to self-realisation is due largely to myopia and free riding. We now see that the same two obstacles arise in the path towards socialism. I believe that the two problems and the solutions to them are closely related, but that is the topic of another paper.[59]

[58]For the idea of counteradaptive preferences, see Elster, *Sour Grapes*, p. 111–12. For the idea that capitalism and socialism cyclically generate desires for each other, see John Dunn, *The Politics of Socialism* (Cambridge University Press, 1984).
[59]See Elster, 'Weakness of Will'.

9 Public ownership and private property externalities

John E. Roemer

9.1 Why public ownership?

If capitalist property relations are ones of private and unequal ownership in the means of production, why should socialist property relations not be ones of private and equal ownership? Why should the negation of capitalist property relations require the abolition of private property (in the means of production), and not simply its redistribution – perhaps once and for all, perhaps in a rather continuous fashion through taxation, perhaps through inheritance taxes once each generation? Socialist theory has been practically universal in its condemnation of private property as an institution – not simply the particular distribution of it that exists in capitalist societies. (Even syndicalism, which calls for cooperative ownership of property by small groups, does not endorse simple private ownership, although the property relations it recommends are to be distinguished from what we think of as public ownership.)

The so-called second theorem of welfare economics states that, under appropriate conditions, any efficient allocation of resources and final output can be achieved by some initial private distribution of property, followed by market trading to equilibrium. That is, any efficient allocation is supported by (Walrasian) equilibrium prices associated with some initial distribution of assets. Given this fact, one is prompted to ask: Is the opposition to private property and markets a kind of socialist Ludditism, in which the institution of property-cum-markets is blamed for the inequality which is associated not with that institution per se, but rather with the initial inequality of the asset distribution? Even more ba-

I thank Louis Makowski for discussions on the topic of Section 9.2. This chapter was written in 1985. For development of the author's views on public ownership since then, see Roemer (1988).

sically, one must ask: What *is* public ownership of the means of production? Surely a desideratum of the final allocation of resources achieved by public ownership is efficiency; but since any efficient allocation is a Walrasian one with respect to some private distribution of assets, what can public ownership do that private ownership cannot do? How should one even define the allocation mechanism associated with 'public ownership'? Will public ownership, whatever it is, not eventually boil down to mimicking some private ownership mechanism, if it is to be efficient?

It may seem naive to pose such a question; for there are at least four reasons, which I will call the standard ones, for socialists' opposition to the private ownership (PrO) mechanism of resource allocation. First, Marxists and others deny the claimed efficiency of the PrO mechanism. In the Marxist story, markets are characterized by anarchy and suboptimal allocations of resources. Where and why does the invisible hand fail? A variety of reasons are given: (a) There are substantial nonconvexities, such as increasing returns to scale and public goods, which nullify the putative benevolence of the market; (b) a complete set of markets does not exist – in particular, futures markets that would be necessary to enable agents to make contingent plans properly under uncertainty – do not exist; (c) monopoly power and market power exist that render the price-taking assumption of competitive equilibrium unrealistic; (d) the economy is indeed never in equilibrium, and the disequilibrium resource allocation properties of a PrO mechanism are bad. Thus, *planning*, an aspect of public ownership (whatever it is), is touted as a device for overcoming the inefficiencies of the market mechanism. The literature on market failure and planning is, of course, voluminous, and it is not my intention to discuss it. Suffice it to say that this first standard reason for opposing the market mechanism is put forward on grounds principally of efficiency, not equity.

The second standard reason for socialist opposition to PrO is that it would have unfair consequences, even if suitable lump-sum transfers of transferable assets were made so that the new socialist economy started off with an appropriately clean slate. That unfairness is due to the impossibility of, in fact, creating a clean slate; for people have certain *preferences* and *skills* that are the legacy of capitalism, in particular, of capitalism's unfair distribution of the means of production. With regard to preferences: Some people have learned to save under capitalism and to train themselves in ways that are conducive to success in any system using PrO as an allocation mechanism. Other people have learned behaviour, values and preferences that are dysfunctional or maladapted to success in a PrO society, even though they lived in such a society. One might argue that their behaviour was well adapted to surviving on the margins of a society so organised, but not to succeeding in the mainstream of that society. With regard to skills: Some people have learned skills, through education, on which they can capitalise in any PrO society, but their acquisition of those skills may have been due to the unfair advantages they enjoyed under capitalism. For these reasons, since preferences and skills are not redistributed or transformed with the 'new slate' of property created in the hypothetical society we are discussing, PrO with initial equal distribution of capital (let us say) does not appropriately right the wrongs of capitalism.

The third standard reason for opposing PrO is on grounds of preference endogeneity. I have referred in the paragraph above to preference endogeneity; but now I mean endogeneity with respect to the kinds of preferences we think people *should* have. The preferences and values people adopt are, surely, to some extent a function of the allocation mechanism itself. Thus private property and markets, it is claimed, generate commodity fetishism. In a regime using PrO, people tend to be evaluated on the basis of the value of their marketable assets, rather than as persons. Women, for example, are undervalued by societies using PrO so long as the raising of children is women's work and unpaid work. This reason for opposing the PrO mechanism is typically socialist and nonliberal: It is socialist in its denial of an essential unchangeable human nature, and it is nonliberal in its readiness to pass judgement on the *quality* of values that people may hold. In the Marxist canon, it is indexed under the topics of alienation and self-realisation or self-actualisation.

The fourth standard reason for opposing the PrO mechanism is, in a sense, the most radical. Even if the values and preferences of people were autonomously formed, or worthy of the effective respect that the PrO mechanism provides them, and even if skills and talents were respectable in that sense as well, there might be opposition to PrO on grounds that people do not deserve, or have a right to, the returns to their internal talents that the market system provides them. The distribution of talents is, after all, morally arbitrary. If that is so, perhaps the distributive consequences of the market system are unfair, even with an initial equal division, let us say, of transferable assets. The market system rewards unequal talent unequally; perhaps some such inequality is necessary for the sake of efficiency, but not so much as the market system may implement. The fourth standard reason differs from the second reason, for the second ruled against only those skills and talents that were specifically the legacy of capitalism's unequal opportunities. The fourth reason argues against self-ownership as a principle. The relative unimportance of the fourth reason in socialist theory is due, I think, to the historic task of socialism, which is to eliminate the unequal distribution of the means of production. It has been viewed either that (a) with the successful abolition of capitalism's unequal opportunities, differences in internal talents and preferences will be eliminated, so that unequal talents are indeed a specifically capitalist problem, or that (b) the inequalities in distribution due to differential talent are of second order in their importance relative to the consequences of differential capital, or that (c) socialism allows differential reward for talent for reasons of incentives. But today the fourth reason emerges more sharply, both due to contemporary political philosophy (e.g., Rawls, 1971; Dworkin, 1981a,b; Barry, 1985), which is concerned with unequal distribution of all morally arbitrary traits, and due to those inequalities in socialist countries that are associated with the limited but increasing use of the PrO mechanism.

It need hardly be said that a new interest in these questions is motivated by market socialism, as it currently expands its domain in socialist countries.

Although plenty of fuel may be provided by the four standard reasons (and, indeed, I surely have missed several important standard reasons, and my reasons could be more finely drawn with a variety of subcases) for a cost–benefit analysis of the PrO mechanism, I wish to propose in this chapter a fifth reason for opposing the PrO mechanism. There are certain negative externalities associated with private ownership mechanisms. I will describe these externalities in the second and third sections, but here I wish to explain why I find it necessary to take what readers may consider to be a pedantic approach. I have already mentioned various negative externalities associated with the use of markets: those of the conventional kind (which are included in the first standard reason), when markets cause harm to some people because property rights in certain assets (such as air) are not delineated or because of production and consumption externalities of familiar kinds. The kinds of preferences that markets induce (the third standard reason) can also be thought of as a negative externality. But the private property externalities I discuss below are in a sense more fundamental than these. They exist even when the most stringent and 'conservative' assumptions are postulated to describe the environment under consideration. I will assume that preferences are exogenous and fixed; that no production of consumption externalities exist; that people have a right to returns on their talents and skills; and that these talents and skills are given before our investigation begins. Under these conditions, a negative externality is nevertheless associated with the private ownership mechanism. Even those quite critical of laissez faire for various of the four standard reasons would agree that the environment depicted in Sections 9.2 and 9.3 is ideal for the market mechanism. Exposing this private property externality will provide a partial answer to one of the questions posed at the beginning of this chapter. Whatever resource allocation implements public ownership, one might require it not to suffer this kind of externality.

Before proceeding, we must add a caveat. My purpose is not to argue against the use of markets in socialism. Indeed, I think that markets, to perhaps a large degree, are beneficial and necessary. I wish to understand what public ownership means and what might justify the apparent Ludditism with respect to the PrO mechanism I have referred to. To this end, I find appropriate the methodologically conservative approach adopted in this chapter.

9.2 Public ownership of transferable assets

How can one conceive of a mechanism that respects both the principle of public ownership with respect to the means of production and private ownership with respect to talents or internal resources? Are there any distributions of the social product that will respect everyone's rights with respect to his participation in the public ownership of the means of production, yet infringe on no one's rights with respect to appropriation of the returns to his private talents? Perhaps these two principles are not consistent. This question is posed and discussed in two papers by Cohen (1986a,b). His work suggests to me the formal approach taken in this section.

In particular, could we implement the goal of (a) public ownership of the means of production and (b) private ownership of skills and labour by use of a market mechanism, following from some initial distribution of the means of production as private property? Such an implementation might be thought of as 'market socialism'.

I suggest an axiomatic approach to studying the kinds of allocations that might implement a notion of public ownership of the means of production, yet respect private ownership of skills, talents and preferences. The approach begins by defining a class of *environments*, consisting of agents with skills and preferences, of resources used in producing the goods that are consumed and of production functions that combine the resources to produce goods. An environment is a pre-economy because no mechanism is specified for resource allocation in the definition of an environment.

Upon the class of environments, mechanisms can be defined that assign to any environment a feasible allocation for that environment. An example of such a mechanism is the Walrasian allocation associated with a certain initial distribution of the resources – say, with an initial equal per capita distribution of resources. A mechanism is a function from the class of environments to their sets of feasible allocations. By requiring certain postulates to be satisfied by the mechanism, we can limit the class of mechanisms to one that implements a notion of public ownership of the means of production, for example.

For the sake of exposition and simplicity, consider a class of environments consisting of just two people and a productive resource called land. These two have, in general, different degrees of skill, s^1 and s^2. We might call them Able and Infirm, after Cohen (1986a,b), for sharpness. Land and labour are used to produce a consumable good, corn, according to the production function $f(W, L)$, where W and L are the inputs of land and labour. The skill levels s^i of the agents measure the labour they can supply in efficiency units. Thus if agent i expends L^i days of labour and agent j expends L^j days of labour on amount W of land, total production of corn will be $f(W, s^1L^1 + s^2L^2)$. Each agent has the same utility function, let us suppose, for corn and leisure, $u(\text{corn, leisure})$. These are the only two goods. Suppose there is an amount of land $\overline{W}$ and each agent is endowed with 1 unit of leisure that can, at will, be converted into labour. All corn must be produced by working the land. An environment $\mathcal{E}$ is now specified: It is a vector $\mathcal{E} = \langle \overline{W}; u; f; s^1, s^2 \rangle$. Given an environment $\mathcal{E}$, the problem is to decide what allocations of corn and labour to the agents will respect two principles: their public ownership of the land and their private ownership of their skills.

An *allocation* is a vector $\langle (C^1, 1 - L^1), (C^2, 1 - L^2) \rangle$ of corn and leisure (or labour) assignments to the two agents. Let the set of feasible allocations for the environment $\mathcal{E}$ be called $\Omega(\mathcal{E})$. An *allocation mechanism F* is a mapping that, to every environment $\mathcal{E}$, assigns a feasible allocation in $\Omega(\mathcal{E})$. Write $F^i(\mathcal{E}) = (C^i, 1 - L^1)$ for the assignment of corn and leisure to individual i under mechanism F.

In the following, let $\mathcal{E}$ and $\mathcal{E}'$ be two environments, where

$$\mathcal{E} = \langle \overline{W}; u; f; s^1, s^2 \rangle \qquad \text{and} \qquad \mathcal{E}' = \langle \overline{W}'; u'; f'; s^{1\prime}, s^{2\prime} \rangle.$$

I suggest a mechanism respecting the two principles of public ownership of the land and private ownership of skills should satisfy the following axioms:

1. *Unrestricted domain (UD).* F is defined on a domain of environments $\mathcal{E}$, where u can be any concave utility function, f can be any constant-returns-to-scale production function and $\overline{W}$, s^1, s^2 can be any non-negative numbers.
2. *Pareto optimality (PO).* $F(\mathcal{E})$ is a Pareto-optimal allocation in $\Omega(\mathcal{E})$.
3. *Land monotonicity (LM).* Let $\mathcal{E}'$ and $\mathcal{E}$ differ only in that $\overline{W}' > \overline{W}$. Then $u(F^i(\mathcal{E}')) \geq u(F^i(\mathcal{E}))$ for $i = 1, 2$.
4. *Absence of negative externalities (ANE).* Let $s^1 \geq s^2$. Then:
   4a. $u(F^2(\overline{W}; u; f; s^1, s^2)) \geq u(F^2(\overline{W}; u; f; s^2, s^2))$ (i.e., Infirm does not suffer because of Able's ability).
   4b. $u(F^1(\overline{W}; u; f; s^1, s^2)) \leq u(F^1(\overline{W}; u; f; s^1, s^1))$ (i.e., Able does not gain by virtue of Infirm's weakness).
5. *Technological monotonicity (TM).* Let $\mathcal{E}'$ and $\mathcal{E}$ differ only in that $f'(W, L) \geq f(W, L)$, $\forall(W, L)$. Then $u(F^i(\mathcal{E}')) \geq u(F^i(\mathcal{E}))$ for $i=1, 2$.
6. *Self-ownership of skill (SO).* In $\mathcal{E}$, suppose $s^i \geq s^j$. Then $u(F^i(\mathcal{E})) \geq u(F^j(\mathcal{E}))$.
7. *Continuity (C).* F is a continuous function, in the appropriate topology, in all its arguments.

Call an F that satisfies Axioms 1–7 *acceptable.*

Axiom 1 says the mechanism F must be a general rule that can work for 'all' environments. Axiom 2 is easily justified (although for technical reasons one might wish to weaken the axiom to require only weak Pareto optimality). Axioms 3 and 5 embody the principle of public ownership of external resources.

As the external resource $\overline{W}$ or the knowledge f improves, neither agent should be hurt. Whatever public ownership means, one can claim it means *at least* what Axioms 3 and 5 require. Axiom 6 embodies self-ownership of skill.

Axiom 4 ensures that the Infirm (Able) agent not suffer (gain) a negative (positive) externality by virtue of the Able (Infirm) agent's ability (infirmity). For instance, Axiom 4a says that Infirm should not end up worse off than he would be in a world where both agents were as unskilled as he. Axiom 4b, similarly, prevents Able from being better off than he would be in a world where Infirm were as skilled as he. What is the justification for these axioms, from our two basic principles of self-ownership and public ownership of the means of production? I am not sure. I find them attractive axioms, and perhaps justifiable from the two basic principles. Indeed, Axiom 4a is more attractive than 4b. Axiom 4b might be unattractive for this reason: Why deny Able a windfall gain so long as it is not taken at Infirm's expense? But Axiom 4a does seem to protect Infirm's property right in himself and his joint ownership of the land with Able.

These axioms are not as parsimonious as they might be. For instance, Axiom 4b implies Axiom 4a if the production function exhibits constant returns to scale.[1] And land monotonicity is a special case of technological monotonicity, so Axiom 3 need not be assumed if Axiom 5 is. I give these axioms as examples of how one might analyse the problem at hand.

Axiom 6 is a self-ownership axiom, as it says that the more skilled person gets at least as much utility as the less skilled. One cannot but benefit from being skillful. Note that Axiom 6 assumes interpersonal comparability of utility. In particular, it implies *symmetry*, that if $s^1 = s^2$ then $u(F^1(\mathcal{E})) = u(F^2(\mathcal{E}))$. Equally skilled agents are treated equally with respect to welfare. Axiom 7 is strong, and I think it would be an error to view it as merely technical. It can be justified by saying that the mechanism should not change its prescription much due to small measurement errors.

The axiomatic approach takes an outcome-oriented rather than a procedural approach towards the issue of public ownership. A procedural approach would specify a political mechanism by which society chooses its leaders, who would then have the authority to decide upon the allocation of social resources. But at some point, an outcome-oriented definition of public ownership would be required, for society's chosen leaders will require criteria by which to allocate resources. My claim is that axioms like the above must be satisfied by any rule that the planners adopt to implement public ownership of the land while respecting private ownership of skills.

One can question these *particular* axioms as ones that capture the requirements of public ownership. I propose, nevertheless, that one can discuss the problem usefully by studying the mechanisms that satisfy these axioms and by perturbing the axioms in ways which that study will suggest.

Given this axiomatisation, it is possible to ask whether certain mechanisms are acceptable. Preeminent among these candidates is the mechanism competitive equilibrium from equal division (ED-CE), which assigns equal property rights in the land to both agents, assigns full

---

[1] I thank A. Hylland for noticing this.

property rights in each agent's labour to himself and allocates corn and labour according to the associated competitive equilibrium. I asked in Section 9.1 why the equal-division mechanism was not an appropriate answer to capitalist inequality. One answer is provided now: ED-CE violates several of the listed axioms. In particular, it violates Axiom 3, land monotonicity. For certain environments, as the amount of land increases, the utility of the less skilled agent decreases in the equal-division allocation.

Briefly, this can happen as follows. Suppose one agent is much more skilled than the other, $s^1 > s^2$. The land $\overline{W}$ is equally divided between the two of them. At the equilibrium, Able is working on his land and is also renting land from Infirm. Perhaps Infirm is not working at all, because his productivity is so low that he is better off collecting rents from Able than working himself. Thus Infirm is living, in large part, or even entirely, on the rents he collects from Able. Now let the amount of land increase.

According to ED-CE, it is again equally divided between the two. They are both apparently wealthier in real endowments. But now, due to the increased amount of land, the marginal productivity of Able's labour is larger if he works all the land. It is possible to design utility functions that will cause Able to decrease his corn consumption and increase his leisure consumption compared with what happened in the first environment. In fact, this will be the case if, at Able's level of wealth, corn is an inferior good and he decreases his consumption of it as his wealth rises. The consequence of his decreasing his own corn consumption can be that the rental value of a unit of land will fall, and even that Infirm's total rents will fall, compared with what he collected from Able in the first environment. Thus Able has become better off in terms of welfare with the increased land in the world, but Infirm has become worse off. Public ownership of land is therefore violated by the ED-CE mechanism, if public ownership entails land monotonicity. There is a *private property externality* that works to the detriment of Infirm. It is a pecuniary externality, an effect that someone suffers because of a change in relative prices due to a change in the aggregate endowment of the economy.

The same private property externality can be generated with the ED-CE mechanism by an improvement in the technology. This is obvious, since formally, increasing the amount of land as was done in the previous example can be viewed as improving the technology. (Imagine, i.e., a land-augmenting technical change that improves the productivity of land rather than increasing its physical quantity.)

This private externality, not surprisingly, can also appear when one agent's skill increases. The ED-CE mechanism violates Axiom 4b in conjunction with Axiom 6. This is seen as follows: Suppose we are given any environment $\mathcal{E}$ with $s^1 > s^2$. Compare it with an environment $\mathcal{E}'$, where both agents have skill s^1, and otherwise things are the same. Under ED-CE, the land is divided equally between the two agents, and in $\mathcal{E}'$ there will be no trade: By symmetry, each will work up his part of the land as much as he likes. Now examine ED-CE in $\mathcal{E}$. The agents start off with one-half the land each, but in general there will be trade; in general, Able will rent some land from Infirm. Thus Able must end up better off under ED-CE in $\mathcal{E}$ than he did in $\mathcal{E}'$, for an option he has in $\mathcal{E}$ is to work up his land and not trade, as he did in $\mathcal{E}'$. By revealed preference Able has gained, under ED-CE, from Infirm's infirmity, a violation of Axiom 4.

I have not, at this writing (1985), characterised exactly the class of mechanisms that satisfy the stated axioms. We see, at least, that one of the most attractive private property mechanisms is not admissible – equal division of the land. At least one mechanism is acceptable: Assign that allocation of corn and labour to the agents that is Pareto optimal and equalises their utilities. (Some additional domain assumption, such as free disposal of utility, is required to guarantee that an equal utility allocation always exists.) Perhaps on a suitably unrestricted domain of economies there is no other acceptable mechanism.[2]

More generally than the equal-division mechanism, one can examine the following class of private ownership mechanisms. Begin with some initial allocation of the land between the two agents, and pass to the Walrasian allocation. It can be shown that any fixed allocation of land (say, give fraction λ to the Able agent and fraction $1 - \lambda$ to Infirm) violates Axioms 3, 4 and 5 on an unrestricted domain of environments. More generally still, one can specify the fraction of the land assigned as property to the more skilled agent as a function of all the other parameters of the economy, that is, view λ as a function of λ $(s^1, s^2, \overline{W})$, for fixed utility and production functions. Now pass to competitive equilibrium. If the function $\lambda(\ )$ is specified, this becomes a mechanism, and we can ask whether a function λ exists that makes the associated mechanism acceptable.

First, one must inquire whether this mechanism strains the conception

[2]In Moulin and Roemer (in press), it is proved that the equal utility mechanism is the unique one satisfying the axioms.

of a private ownership mechanism; for if the skill of an agent increases, or if the amount of land increases or the technology changes, we must change the initial allocation of the resource in the 'private ownership' economy. We are, in fact, trying to cook the 'private' distribution of property to conform to our 'public' requirements. What these mechanisms must in general do is assign an increasingly large fraction of the land to the infirm agent as the skill of the able one increases. I think there is no interesting sense in which such a mechanism can be considered a private ownership one. But there is a prior point of rebuttal against such mechanisms. It may be that the only assignment of property that respects the various monotonicity axioms requires, for some economies, that some of Able's *leisure* be given as property to Infirm. Thus Infirm would own one unit of his own leisure, all the land, and some fraction of Able's leisure. Barring the redistribution of Able's leisure in this fashion, Infirm's welfare would decrease as, for example, the amount of land increased beyond a certain amount. While this redistribution of Able's leisure property right would not necessarily violate any of the listed axioms, it would violate an obvious additional requirement we might impose for self-ownership within the class of private ownership mechanisms – namely, that no property right in a person's labour should ever be assigned to another person.

To summarise, I have argued that whatever public ownership of the means of production means, it should at least guarantee that no one's welfare decreases as the amount of the publicly owned resource increases, ceteris paribus. Whatever private ownership of self means, it should at least mean the 'absence of negative externalities in skill' and also that if Able has more of the talent in question than does Infirm, then Able should fare at least as well as Infirm in the allocation assigned by the mechanism. Other than for the necessary conditions, the axioms are agonostic concerning precisely how to balance the competing claims of the public and private spheres. The conclusion is that all private ownership mechanisms fail to respect what might be considered this minimalist constitution of public ownership. Private ownership mechanisms suffer upon certain agents a negative externality that, in a sense, renders all traits 'social'.

9.3 Public ownership of talents

In the preceding section I argued that even a moderately conservative program, of seeking to implement public ownership of alienable assets while respecting private ownership of inalienable resources, called talents, might mandate a surprisingly welfare-egalitarian constitution. In particular, the market mechanism starting from equal division of worldly resources would violate requirements of that program. There is a pecuniary externality which I called a private ownership externality that makes it difficult to separate neatly the public and private spheres. There are spillover effects from the private ownership of some goods that impinge on the rights of public ownership of some agents.

I did not characterise the class of mechanisms that satisfy the two principles of public ownership of land and private ownership of talent in the preceding section. I suggested that it may be the case that, on a sufficiently unrestricted domain, private ownership of talent is moot, in the sense that the only acceptable mechanism might equalise welfares. If this is the case, there would be little motivation to propose any further chipping away of the privately owned sphere. It may, however, be the case that acceptable mechanisms (other than welfare egalitarianism) exist for the model described here, in which case one could be motivated to ask what it would mean to require public ownership of *all* resources, whether they be alienable, like land, or inalienable, like skills. This is a distinctly more radical program than the one in Section 9.2. It could be motivated by several of the standard objections of Section 9.1 (namely, the ones which maintain that all talents and attributes are morally arbitrary, and hence those who are born with them should have no private claims on the returns they can earn). Certainly, contemporary egalitarian political philosophy has adopted this position in part: I refer, for example, to the distributional proposals of Rawls (1971) and Dworkin (1981a,b). I have investigated this question in more detail in Roemer (1985, 1986).

In this section, I show how private property externalities emerge when we extend property rights to cover 'personal' assets like talents and attributes. Suppose one wants to implement public ownership of talent. One might think that an appropriate way to redistribute the returns from personally held talents is to distribute the property rights in a person's talent to many different people and then to use markets to arrive at a Pareto-optimal allocation. The motivation for proposing this extended private ownership mechanism is the same one as before: Since any efficient allocation can be achieved by some initial distribution of all assets, now including personal ones, perhaps a 'market' solution to the program of radical public ownership could be attractive. But I will show that externalities continue to exist which render such a solution unpalatable.

Just as it has been shown that the Marxist negation of 'unequal owner-ship of the means of production' is not 'equal but private ownership of the means of production', so this section shows that the morally appro-priate negation of 'private and unequal ownership of talents' is not 'pri-vate and equal ownership of talents'.

To see the issues involved, consider the following model, of two peo-ple who have the same preferences for corn and leisure $u(\text{corn, leisure})$ but different skills s^1 and s^2. Since alienable assets are not the issue here, I simplify the model of the preceding section by assuming that corn is produced from labour alone, without land. Agent i can produce s^i units of corn with one unit of his labour. Each agent is endowed with one unit of leisure, which can be converted into labour to produce corn.

Consider what allocation equal-division competitive equilibrium would give rise to in this world, where the 'resources' to be equally divided between the agents are their skills. An apparently obvious way of accomplishing this kind of equalisation is to assign each person equal property rights in everyone's leisure. Thus each agent owns one-half of his own leisure, in this model, and one-half of the other's leisure – val-ued, of course, at their market prices. Corn has a price of 1, and no corn exists at the beginning; all of it must be produced. In equilibrium each agent maximises utility subject to his budget constraint, and the supply of corn produced by the labour of the agents is just equal to the total demand for corn. Agent 1 chooses (C^1, L^1), a corn–leisure bundle, to

$$\max u(C^1, L^1),$$
$$\text{s.t.} \quad C^1 + s^1L^1 = \tfrac{1}{2}s^1 + \tfrac{1}{2}s^2.$$

Agent 2 chooses (C^2, L^2) to

$$\max u(C^2, L^1),$$
$$\text{s.t.} \quad C^2 + s^2L^2 = \tfrac{1}{2}s^1 + \tfrac{1}{2}s^2.$$

Equilibrium requires

$$C^1 + C^2 = s^1(1-L^1) + s^2(1-L^2).$$

In the model, the price of corn is set at unity, and in equilibrium the price of a unit of labour of agent i will be exactly its marginal value product, s^i. It is easy to illustrate the consequences of the above equal division in skills equilibrium, as shown in Figure 9.1. Notice that the two agents have the same wealth; but the left-hand sides of their budget constraints differ in that the skilled agent has to buy back his expensive leisure, while the unskilled agent is fortunate enough to enjoy consuming cheap

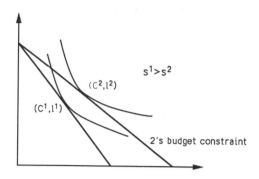

$s^1 > s^2$

(c^2, l^2)

(c^1, l^1)

2's budget constraint

Fig. 9.1 Utilities of two agents with equal division of skills.

leisure. Thus at the equilibrium, the skilled agent will be worse off in welfare terms than the unskilled. Hence this mechanism for achieving equal opportunities in skills penalises the skilled agent.[3]

The source of this anomaly has been alluded to. Once property rights in each person's skills are distributed equally to all, the skilled agent is like a person with an expensive taste. He has the unfortunate handicap of liking a scarce good with a high price. He is unable to consume cheap leisure and must consume expensive leisure. These two agents do not, in fact, have *identical* preferences, as I assumed. They have preferences over different goods. There are three goods in this model: corn, 1's leisure, and 2's leisure. Agent 1 likes corn and 1's leisure, and agent 2 likes corn and 2's leisure.

Not only is there an obvious ethical problem with the equal-division-of-skills mechanism, but there is an implementation problem. The mechanism is not incentive compatible. The skilled person has an incentive to lie about his skill, to perform below his capability, since his final welfare is monotone decreasing in his reported skill level. The informational requirements necessary to implement this mechanism (namely, that people's skills can be properly diagnosed) are inconsistent with the reason one might be led to use markets in the first place – namely, to decentralise resource allocation.

But this failure of incentive compatibility is not my concern here. I am investigating the equal-division mechanism for its properties in implementing a public ownership ethic, not for its usefulness as a decentralising mechanism. From the radical public ownership point of view,

[3]Note that this welfare comparison assumes interpersonally comparable utility, although the equal-division mechanism does not require such an assumption.

what seems objectionable about the above result is not that the skilled agent ends up with lower utility than the unskilled, but rather that they end up with different utilities. We think of the two agents as having identical preferences, although in fact they do not, because their leisures are different goods. It would seem that, in this environment, the only ethically appropriate way of implementing public ownership with respect to skill is to assign the allocation that equalises welfare, since the agents differ only with regard to skill. Intuitively, the sense in which these two agents have different tastes (i.e., tastes for personalised leisure) does not comprise a morally relevant difference. Our ED-CE mechanism, which views the leisures as different goods, does not discriminate as does our moral intuition.

The essential characteristic of the economy just described is not, as it may appear, associated with production, but rather with the fact that one agent has an expensive taste. To clarify this point, I present a second model in which public ownership can be investigated, in which production is absent but the expensive-taste feature remains. Imagine that there are two people, Andrea and Bob, and three goods: rice, beer and champagne (R, B, and C). Andrea likes rice and beer, and Bob likes rice and champagne, but their preferences over rice and alcohol are identical. Thus Andrea's utility is $u(R, B)$ and Bob's is $u(R, C)$. Andrea gets no kick from champagne, and Bob gets none (too bad for him, as we shall see) from beer. The aggregate endowments of the three goods are $\overline{R}$, $\overline{B}$, and $\overline{C}$, and $\overline{C} < \overline{B}$. Champagne is a scarce good. In an equal-division world, we divide up all the property equally between the two people and examine the associated Walrasian equilibrium. Thus each of Andrea and Bob receives an endowment of $.5\overline{R}$, $.5\overline{B}$ and $.5\overline{C}$. Let the equilibrium price of rice be 1 and the prices of beer and champagne be, respectively, p_B and p_C. Then at equilibrium Andrea chooses R^1 and B^1 to

$$\max u(R^1, B^1),$$
$$\text{subject to} \quad R^1 + p_B B^1 = .5\overline{R} + .5p_B\overline{B} + .5p_C\overline{C},$$

and Bob chooses R^2 and C^2 to

$$\max u(R^2, C^2),$$
$$\text{subject to} \quad R^2 + p_C C^2 = .5\overline{R} + .5p_B\overline{B} + .5p_C\overline{C}.$$

Equilibrium prices clear markets:

$$R^1 + R^2 = \overline{R},$$
$$B^1 = \overline{B},$$
$$C^2 = \overline{C}.$$

I have written the problem so that it is clear that Andrea ends up getting all the beer and Bob all the champagne. It must be this way, since the equilibrium is Pareto optimal, and any other allocation of beer and champagne would be suboptimal, since Andrea and Bob get a kick only from their respective kinds of alcohol.

It is not difficult to show, in this model, that the equilibrium price of champagne is higher than the price of beer, since champagne is relatively scarce, and the preferences of the agents are appropriately symmetric. For certain utility functions, it is the case that Andrea will have a higher welfare at equilibrium than Bob. Andrea and Bob have the same income, but he likes a good with a high price. It may cost her less to purchase the large quantity $\overline{B}$ than it costs him to purchase the smaller quantity $\overline{C}$.[4]

But there is a further unpleasantness with the equal-division mechanism. One might say that since only Andrea likes beer, and only Bob likes champagne, let us give all the beer to Andrea and all the champagne to Bob, simply divide the rice equally between them and let them trade to equilibrium. Indeed, no trade will take place since no Pareto improvements are possible from that allocation. Each ends up with one-half the stock of rice and all of the kind of alcohol that he or she likes. Now suppose one thought the equal-division-of-everything mechanism was an appropriate way of implementing public ownership of everything. When each has one-half the rice, and all of his or her personalized type of alcohol, Andrea is clearly better off than Bob, because she is consuming more beer than he is champagne, and they have the same preferences for their respective alcohols.

That is, $u(.5\overline{R},\overline{B}) > u(.5\overline{R},\overline{C})$. Let us, then, compare this allocation with the one arrived at in the previous paragraphs, where $\overline{R}$, $\overline{C}$, and $\overline{B}$ are divided equally between Andrea and Bob initially, and they pass to competitive equilibrium. The result is that Bob is *even worse off* with the full equal-division mechanism than he is when only the rice was divided in half. (In the full equal-division equilibrium, he may end up with less than one-half the rice, although he always gets all the champagne.) Hence in our attempt to compensate Bob for his unfortunate taste for champagne, by applying the equal-division mechanism to all goods, we may render him even worse off than when we did not extend the jurisdiction of the mechanism to those resources with respect to which the agents' preferences differ.

[4]See Roemer (1985) for the details of this example.

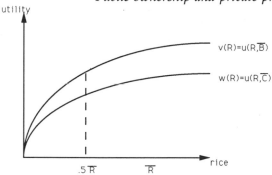

utility

$v(R)=u(R,\overline{B})$

$w(R)=u(R,\overline{C})$

.5$\overline{R}$ $\overline{R}$ rice

Fig. 9.2 Andrea's and Bob's utilities for rice.

Perhaps the reader has little sympathy for Bob, since his taste for champagne may seem to be something for which society need not compensate him. But that objection is not convincing, since preferences here are exogenous and involuntary; Bob does not have an expensive taste because he cultivated it. To make this point sharply, consider a variation of the Andrea–Bob story. Andrea and Bob get apparently different cardinal, interpersonally comparable utility from rice. Andrea's utility function is $v(R)$ and Bob's is $w(R)$. Andrea gets more kick from rice than Bob: For all R, $v(R) > w(R)$, as in Figure 9.2. Public ownership of the observable resource, according to the equal-division procedure, would assign each of them one-half the rice, as illustrated. Now suppose we discover that the reason Andrea and Bob have different utility from rice is that each is consuming another good, called endorphins. Andrea and Bob in fact have identical preferences over rice *and* endorphins, but Andrea has a higher level of endorphins than Bob. In fact, their common utility function for rice and endorphins is $u(R,E)$, where u is the same utility function discussed immediately above. Andrea has an amount of endorphins, given to her by nature, labelled $\overline{B}$, and Bob's endorphin level is $\overline{C}$, where as stated $\overline{C} > \overline{B}$.

If we apply the equal-division-of-all-resources mechanism, we divide up the property rights in rice and endorphins so that each owns, initially, one-half the rice, $.5\overline{R}$, and one-half of everyone's endorphins. Thus Andrea and Bob each gets an initial endowment of $(.5\overline{R},\ .5\overline{B},\ .5\overline{C})$. They now trade to equilibrium. In equilibrium, there will be a high price for Bob's scarce endorphins and a low price for Andrea's plentiful ones, and each will repurchase all of the endorphins that he or she alone can consume. The model is formally identical to the beer–champagne model, although the story changes our moral perceptions, perhaps. As I wrote, it is entirely possible (depending on the utility function u) that Bob will end up even worse off under the full equal-division mechanism than he does when the rice is divided equally between the two of them, and no effort is made to compensate him for his unlucky endorphin endowment.

If this happens, I say that the mechanism behaves *inconsistently* when it is required to include more goods within the jurisdiction of public ownership. Elsewhere, I have given a formal definition of consistency of allocation mechanisms (Roemer, 1986).

The moral of these stories is that, even disregarding the problems of revelation and incentive compatibility, the equal-division mechanism is not an attractive one for implementing public ownership; for if public ownership were so conceived, extending the jurisdiction of publicly owned goods from rice, to rice and endorphins, could render even worse off the person whom public ownership presumably should compensate. If we view public ownership of talents, whatever it is, as seeking to provide increased welfare for those with an initially paltry endowment of talent, then 'nationalizing' the stocks of the endowment in question should not render those unfortunate persons even worse off. In this example, extending the jurisdiction of the equal-division mechanism to those resources that are unequally (genetically) endowed may harm the people we wish to help. The reason is that, although we can divide up property rights in assets that are metaphysically inseparable from particular agents, in which case these agents will have to repurchase those assets at the equilibrium prices, we cannot equalize their differential preferences, the fact that they like different goods. Bob can consume only his endorphins and Andrea can consume only hers, and there is no way to alter the relative scarcity of his. Although the preferences of the two agents seem, in the relevant ethical sense, to be the same over rice and endorphins, they are in fact unalterably different.

My conclusion is, qualitatively, the same as the conclusion of the preceding section. There is a private property externality that renders the equal-division mechanism, extended to a domain of inalienable assets, inappropriate for implementing public ownership.[5] Competitive mar-

---

[5] In fact, the pecuniary externality of 'inconsistency' exhibited here is related to the externality of Section 9.2. What I showed was that an increase in the amount of land, for example, could reduce the welfare of one of the agents, when the land is equally distributed between the agents. In the example with rice and endorphins, imagine that both Bob and Andrea start out with Bob's level of endorphins, $\bar{C}$. Equal division of all goods followed by trading will result in each purchasing his or her endorphins and one-half the rice, in equilibrium. Now suppose that Andrea's endorphin level increases to $\bar{B}$. We divide up

kets, along with an initial equal division of all assets, are not an appropriate mechanism for implementing the goals of public ownership, if public ownership requires at least the kind of welfare monotonicity with respect to increases in the availability of the publicly owned goods that axioms like 'land monotonicity' require, and if it requires the kind of 'consistency' that the equal-division mechanism has here been shown to violate.

Just as Section 9.2 presented an axiomatic characterisation of allocation mechanisms respecting public ownership of the land and private ownership of skill, so it is possible to present an axiomatic characterisation of mechanisms implementing public ownership of all assets, whether they be internal or external. The theorem is: Any mechanism that satisfies several conditions that seem necessary for all resources, internal and external, to be 'publicly owned' must equalise the welfares of the agents (Roemer, 1986). But one does not have to agree that public ownership requires the several axioms of that theorem to endorse the weaker point, made here, that the market mechanism has various unpleasant properties, with respect to monotonicity of welfare and consistency, that render it unsuitable for implementing public ownership.

9.4 Summary

I have been concerned, in this chapter, with what public ownership of assets could mean. Since any efficient allocation of resources can be achieved by the Walrasian mechanism with some private distribution of initial endowments, under suitable assumptions, what could public ownership do that private ownership cannot do? There are various standard answers to this question, which I do not pursue here. My approach is methodologically more conservative, and therefore the criticism of the private ownership–market mechanism that I make is in a sense more fundamental than the standard ones.

I showed that there is an 'externality' associated with the market

property rights in his endorphins, her endorphins, and the rice equally between them. Although Bob may seem initially better off in real terms, the change in relative prices may very well render him worse off in the new equilibrium than he was before – that is, he will end up with all of his own endorphins but perhaps with less than one-half the rice. An increase in the level of one of the 'publicly owned' goods (namely, Andrea's endorphins) renders Bob worse off. This is just the kind of private property externality that was exhibited in Section 9.2. Bob, in this case, suffers a negative externality from Andrea's lavish endowment of endorphins: He is worse off, in the final allocation under equal-division competitive equilibrium, than he would be if Andrea had the same level of endorphins as he.

mechanism that can lead to harming agents whose welfare 'public ownership' is designed to improve. In particular, the kinds of final inequalities associated, in capitalist economies, with initial distributions of assets that are unequal are not necessarily rectified in the right way by beginning with an equal division of all assets. Hence for critics of capitalist inequality, what is called into question is not just the distribution of private property, but the market mechanism based on any distribution of private property.

My intuition is that mechanisms that obey the necessary postulates for public ownership will be considerably more welfare egalitarian in their consequences than private ownership mechanisms are. This does not mean, in practice, that markets cannot be used to implement a conception of public ownership. It means, rather, that there would have to be frequent or continuous redistributions to adjust for the private property externalities that come about from the use of markets. There are, furthermore, many other reasons to use markets that I have not discussed here, including decentralisation.

I claim neither that the arguments presented here constitute a general indictment against the use of markets and private ownership under socialism (as I have made no attempts to analyse the benefits from the market mechanism), nor that these private property externalities constitute the most important negative feature of markets, from a socialist viewpoint. My aim has been more circumscribed: to get some understanding of what the anomalous term 'public ownership' means.

References

Barry, Brian. (1985). *Fair Division and Social Justice*. Unpublished manuscript, California Institute of Technology, Division of Social Science and Humanities.

Cohen, G. A. (1986a). 'Self-Ownership, World Ownership, and Equality'. In F. Lucash (ed.), *Justice and Equality Here and Now*. Ithaca, N.Y.: Cornell University Press.

(1986b). 'Self-Ownership, World-Ownership, and Equality'. *Social Philosophy and Policy* 3: 77–96.

Dworkin, Ronald. (1981a). 'What Is Equality? Part I: Equality of Welfare'. *Philosophy and Public Affairs* 10 (no. 3): 185–246.

(1981b). 'What Is Equality? Part II: Equality of Resources'. *Philosophy and Public Affairs* 10 (no. 4) 283–345.

Moulin, Hervé, and J. Roemer. (In press). 'Public Ownership of the External World and Private Ownership of Self'. *Journal of Political Economy*.

Rawls, John. (1971). *A Theory of Justice*. Cambridge, Mass.: Belknap Press.

Roemer, John E. (1985). 'Equality of Talent'. *Economics and Philosophy 1*: 157–87.
    (1986). 'Equality of Resources Implies Equality of Welfare'. *Quarterly Journal of Economics 101*: 751–84.
    (1988). 'On Public Ownership'. University of California, Davis, Department of Economics Working Paper no. 317.